A PRACTICAL GUIDE FOR BUSINESSWOMEN TRAVELING ALONE

Susanna North

CORNERSTONE LIBRARY
NEW YORK, NEW YORK

Copyright © 1980 by Susanna North
All rights reserved
including the right of reproduction
in whole or in part in any form
Published by Cornerstone Library
A Simon & Schuster Division of
Gulf & Western Corporation
Simon & Schuster Building
1230 Avenue of the Americas
New York, New York 10020

Designed by Irving Perkins
Manufactured in the United States of America
10 9 8 7 6 5 4 3 2 1

"Cornerstone Library" and the cube design are registered trademarks of Cornerstone Library, Inc., a Simon & Schuster subsidiary of Gulf & Western Corporation.

Library of Congress Cataloging in Publication Data

North, Susanna.
  Traveling alone.

  1. Women executives. 2. Women in business.
3. Travel—Handbooks, manuals, etc. I. Title.
HF5500.2.N66   910'.2'4042   79–16926
ISBN 0–671–18442–3
ISBN 0–346–12422–0 pbk.

*For The Kid;
for Boston and Seattle; for San Francisco,
Atlanta and Chicago; for Cincinnati and
for Indiana State Route 35; and for all
the silver cities in between.*

Contents

Introduction	1
1. Prerequisites	5
2. Packing	17
3. Getting There—on the Road	41
4. Getting There—by Air	65
5. Lodging	85
6. Food	93
7. "Table for One, Please"	113
8. Health	131
9. Men	143
10. Conventions, Conferences, and Seminars	169
11. Overseas	175
12. The Corporate Gypsy	191
Index	197

Introduction

More women than ever before are living alone and liking it. More women than ever before are occupying executive-level positions in business. This means that more and more women are doing something that was almost unheard of fifty years ago: they are traveling . . . alone.

Even for women of my generation (born in the 1940s) the phenomenon is relatively new. When my male cousins went roaring off on their motorcycles for a summer in California, they received only faintly worried frowns from their parents; but when my sister and I, also college-age, went off by bus to visit an elderly aunt for the weekend, we were loaded down with cautions about not speaking to strange men and calling home as soon as we arrived. Even today, I am not surprised to find myself the only woman on the commuters' special out of Detroit or Boston on a weekday morning, or the only unaccompanied woman drinking coffee at an all-night Howard-Johnson's-by-the-Freeway.

But I am pleased when I notice that there are other females toting attaché cases through the airport or checking into truckers' motels (which, by the way, are cheaper, friendlier, and more comfortable than the big-name chains). If women are to achieve equal status in business, we must be able to handle a two-day jaunt to Denver or a six-month whistle-stop tour of manufacturing plants with equal aplomb and no visible hassles.

United Airlines recently conducted a survey of business travelers. They found that as of 1978, 16 percent of business travelers are women, compared to 4 percent in 1974 and less than 1 percent in 1970. Here are some more interesting statistics about women travelers, as compared to men*:

	Female	Male
Traveling to attend a convention	39%	12%
Round trips per year	10	18
Through a travel agent	55%	47%
Nights away from home	7	5
Not married	37%	16%
Average age	38	41
Average family income	$25,000	$32,700

I will comment on the significance of these figures later in the book.

* Reprinted courtesy of *Mainliner* magazine carried aboard United Airlines. © 1978 East/West Network, Inc.

United's Vice President of Advertising and Promotion, Fred Heckel, recalled an advertising campaign started in 1967. You may remember it. It featured the "little wife" saying to her traveling husband, "Take me along." He replied, "I love you, little cutie, but the office is my duty." Heckel commented: "If we aired that commercial today, we'd be burned in effigy—or worse." You betcha, Fred.

Women have a number of special problems when they travel alone. The least of these (though one of the most aggravating) is the "You-drove-all-the-way-*by-yourself*?" greeting we often receive. This has to be dealt with, but more serious is the problem of overcoming our own educational and psychological conditioning. Change a flat tire? Carry all those suitcases? Go to a movie alone? Outface an arrogant waiter? Who, me? Even more difficult is the very real problem of safety, which unfortunately must be one of the themes of this book. There are some things that a woman just can't do because they're too dangerous; there are extra precautions she must take and jarring situations she must handle, such as when the hotel clerk loudly announces her room number to a lobby full of half-drunk traveling males.

This is not a book for neophytes. It assumes that you already have a certain amount of sophistication, that you know you're supposed to tip waiters and cab drivers, that you can find out for yourself how to apply for a passport. It contains practical advice, ranging from how to handle overly protective male colleagues, to how to carry on a love affair when you're based in Boston and he's based in Seattle, to how to bluff your way on to a plane when you're seven-months pregnant. It's a book I wished I could have gone out and bought, but it hadn't been written, so I did the next best thing and wrote it myself.

My credentials for writing the book are excellent. I have been traveling alone on business (and not a few vacations) for more than fifteen years. I lived in London for five years and traveled all over Europe. I once circumnavigated the globe (mostly by air) in three weeks. For a year, my job required 100 percent travel: Any belongings that wouldn't fit into the trunk of my car went into storage. I gave up my apartment and set out. In that year I crossed the country five times (twice by road), made some new friends, had several very satisfactory love affairs and kissed too many toads, got lost 182 times but never missed a plane, lost ten pounds but gained a great deal of experience.

In addition to using my own experience, I talked with other women who travel often. My preferred traveling style would not suit everyone. I try to find an apartment to borrow or sublet if I'm staying in a city more than a week, but other women I know prefer the convenience of hotels. I pick up men in airports but not in restaurants, though I know women who do exactly the opposite, and others won't pick up men at all. I like to drive at night and take my chances on finding a motel when I get tired, but some women consider that too risky. I'm perfectly happy to stay in with books to read three evenings in a row, but others go stir crazy if they can't get out to a disco or a nightclub several times a week. The book takes into account differing lifestyles and personal preferences.

1

Prerequisites

I had stopped over in Boston to visit some relatives. I was on my way to Melbourne, Australia. My cousin came to the airport to see me off, and as I was about to get on the plane she asked (being the mother of five teenagers), "Do you have enough money?"

"Oh, sure," I replied. "I have fifteen dollars." And I waved good-bye and got on the plane. About a year later I found out that the story had become a family legend—how I'd gone to Australia with fifteen dollars.

In fact, when I arrived in Melbourne I still had thirteen dollars left. (All my luggage had been left behind at a refueling stop in Honolulu, but that's another story.) Why not? Except for drinks, there's no way to spend money on a plane, and I don't drink on planes. Fifteen dollars was more than enough for magazines, snacks, or other incidental purchases at intermediate stops. I had my checkbook and some credit cards, of course, so I would not have been stranded if something had gone wrong. I knew that our business client would have a car and a driver waiting for me in Melbourne, a cash advance for expense money, and facilities for getting checks cashed and money changed through the office petty-cash department.

Even the delayed luggage was not a disaster. I had essential toilet articles and business papers in my carry-on bag, and I knew from experience that the airline would probably deliver the rest of my belongings to my hotel within a day, which they did. I had planned my arrival for a Friday, so I had the weekend to recover from jet lag; if necessary, I could have gone out and bought an entire wardrobe on Saturday and shown up at the office on Monday rested, clean, well dressed, and calm.

I tell this story to illustrate the three prerequisites for becoming a successful business traveler. They are attitude, planning, and organization.

For women travelers, the right attitude is probably the most important of these, but for some women it is the most difficult to achieve. We have inherited the eighteenth-century notion that travel is a great adventure into the unknown, not to be undertaken without trepidation and the anticipation of hardship and danger. For middle- and upper-class women, travel alone was unthinkable. A Man—one's father or husband—made the arrangements and acted as chaperone and bodyguard. Only upper-class women traveled regularly for pleasure, even as late as the nineteenth century. It is said of Queen Victoria that it came as a great surprise to her, after many years of travel, to learn that you had to *pay* on trains. There was always a retainer who took care of details like tickets.

If a lower-class woman made a long journey, it probably meant one of two things. She may have been a servant, which implied a certain degree of protection. If not that, then she was an immigrant, traveling with her family or alone in steerage class, surrounded by other women. In the latter case, the journey was usually a once-in-a-lifetime occurrence, and a very unpleasant one.

In business today, people who travel often are salespersons or executives. Most of them are men. Secretaries, typists, and other clerical workers just don't get sent on business trips. Most of these workers are women. This is changing, thanks to the Women's Movement and to legislation that is making it necessary for companies to give women management training and promotions. We are still very much a minority, however.

This was brought home to me very recently at a management conference given by my company. Of sixty attendees, three were women. Now, in most business situations the people I am working with know even before meeting me who I am and what my job is. At the conference, however, I was talking with managers from other divisions who had never met me nor been formally introduced to me. At the first coffee break, one man came up to me, looked at my badge, which gave my name and department but not my title, and said, "Oh yes, I've talked with you on the phone quite a lot." Puzzled, I said, "No, I don't think so." I knew I'd never seen him before, and I certainly would have remembered if we'd had frequent phone conversations.

The same thing happened no less than three times that first day, at coffee breaks and lunch. I couldn't figure it out. Why did these guys think they'd had a telephone relationship with me, when I knew it wasn't true? Finally, the light dawned and with it, my anger. They assumed I was the department secretary, the person who answered the phone whenever they called. They *did* talk to her often, but had never bothered to find out her name (nor the fact that she has been going to college at night and is about to get her degree and certification as an accountant—no more typing and phone answering for *her*, either). I spent the rest of the conference in a quiet state of fury, but made damn sure I whipped out my business card to present to anyone who wandered over to chat with me.

Male attitudes like this will probably be the last thing to change. I still find, for example, that a businessman I am visiting will insist on meeting me at the airport, when I know that if I were male he would assume I was perfectly capable of renting a car and finding his office by myself. Which I am, having done it more often than he has, in most cases.

More important than male attitudes, however, are our own attitudes. There is absolutely no reason why you can't rent a car and get there by yourself, and if you don't already feel that way, it's time to change.

If you are a novice business traveler, which most women are, an attitude of independence will be your most important asset. It's not unlikely that you have traveled alone before, but it was probably on vacation, or back and forth from college. Business travel is different in a number of respects.

First of all, on a vacation the travel may be the whole object of the exercise. The purpose of the trip is to go somewhere new, see new things. In business, travel is only incidental. The important things will happen after you get there. This means that travel has to be handled with a minimum of effort and as quickly as possible.

If you're going to Bermuda on vacation, a delay on the trip may be annoying, but it really doesn't matter if you arrive a few hours late. On a business trip, a delay may mean that you lose out on the sale, or miss the meeting altogether, or cause a great deal of inconvenience to others who must change their plans because you're not there. (In fact, this happens quite often; I'll discuss it more a little later.)

On vacation, where you are going and how much it costs are key factors. For a business trip, the destination is not chosen for its climate or tourist amenities. If the conference is in Phoenix, you go to Phoenix and you don't think about how much it's going to cost. The cost is a necessary business expense. What is important is *how long* it will take to get there. Travel time, not miles, is the critical element. This is illustrated over and over again in the chat of business travelers. The trip from Detroit to Chicago is much easier than the trip from Chicago to Detroit. Because of the one-hour time difference, the first trip takes no time at all—you can leave at 8 A.M. and arrive at 8 A.M. But the second trip takes two hours. This is an important consideration; business people based in Detroit can go to Chicago and put in a full day's work; but Chicagoans traveling to Detroit plan either to arrive the night before or start their trip at 6 A.M. Ask a salesperson who travels by car how far it is from Boston to Providence, and she'll tell you it's an hour. Transatlantic travel is based on sun time, too. When it's 1 P.M. in New York it's five hours later, or 6 P.M., in London. The plane journey takes seven hours, which means that London is twelve hours from New York, but New York is two hours from London. You can go from Boston to New York, put in a day's work, and return that evening. To get from Boston to a small town in upper New York State, however, may require four or five hours' travel, because of plane connections. It may not be practical to go and return the same day.

Learning to think in terms of time and convenience instead of distance will probably come automatically when you start to travel regularly. Coping successfully when things don't go as planned may take a little more effort.

This is only the first chapter of the book, and I've already mentioned things that can go wrong several times. On vacation, if your luggage is lost or you get bumped off your flight or if your car breaks down in West Virginia, it may be a major disaster and will certainly be a topic of conversation for a long time to come. But the more you travel, the more you will encounter such crises. Statistically, they must happen, and they do. Such things remain topics of conversation; business travelers can occupy hours of airport waiting time just swapping stories about travel experiences. But for business travelers two things change. One is that you develop a much more philosophical attitude about them, and the second is that you learn to plan to minimize the disruptive effects.

You will develop this attitude in time. You're checked in for the flight and waiting to board, when the loudspeaker clicks on and a tired voice says, "We regret to announce...." You sigh and start getting out your flight guide to find an alternative way to get there.

Learning not to be upset when things go wrong is easier if you know that experienced travelers deal with it all the time. Throughout this book, I'll be giving advice about how to cope with such problems. Let's take just one example here: getting lost. A canceled flight or a flat tire may not be within your control, but surely, an experienced traveler doesn't *get lost*. Let me tell you, they do, often. I've seen a group of senior (male) executives go out to lunch in a strange town and not come back for three hours. They got lost in the mountains. The story sounded highly unlikely, but this was in a remote mountainous area, and I'm sure it was true. Another man I know got on the wrong plane and ended up in Tallahassee, Florida, when he intended to go to Roanoke, Virginia. An ex-boss of mine spent half a day sitting in on the wrong meeting before discovering his error; he should have been at the *other* Sheraton Inn. A software company representative I know showed up at a customer's San Diego office when he was expected in Seattle. (He turned the situation to advantage and made a sale to the San Diego people, then went on to Seattle and made another sale there.) I've been lost in just about every major city in the United States. Well, maybe not really lost—I knew where I was and where I wanted to be, but I couldn't get there.

The attitude of independence, it must be repeated, is your most valuable asset. You *can* cope. No matter what goes wrong, you're resourceful and you'll find a way to manage. Other people do it all the time. Any travel crisis you find yourself in will have happened to others, often. Keeping this in mind when you set out will see you through the worst.

Being independent also means using the resources you have available to you. You *don't* have to face every problem entirely on your own. Because you are on business you have some *juice*; you have an expense account, credit cards, insurance, and an organization behind you. In fact, I believe that women are less likely to use the resources of their organization, partly because they don't like to ask other women—that is, secretaries—to do things for them. But a man would and so should you. This means asking a secretary to make your reservations, run down to Petty Cash for you, get your photocopying done. If you're stranded overnight in a strange city, the cost of the hotel goes on your expense account. If your sales samples are stolen from the room while you're at dinner, you can call the office the next morning and get replacements air-freighted. You have office phones to use to call home to make sure the children are OK. You can ask to have both business and personal messages forwarded by phone.

On this subject, I cannot decide whether the advantages of being female make up for the disadvantages when traveling. The major disadvantage of being a woman traveling alone is that your physical safety is more at risk, and I guess no quantity of small courtesies can make up for that. But when being female gives me an advantage, I use it. I know that earlier in my career, I was denied promotions and raises just because I was female. If my company is now forced by government regulations to give me training and promotions over equally qualified men, I feel not one whit guilty. If there are five of us hanging around the ticket counter trying to get on a flight as stand-by passengers, and I'm offered the single seat because I'm the only woman, I go. If a man gallantly waves me to the head of the line at the car rental counter, I step right up. If attendees at a conference are expected to double up in hotel rooms to keep expenses down, and I get my own room because I'm the only woman, I enjoy every minute of my privacy. If I'm traveling with a man who feels obliged by custom to offer me the choice of the aisle seat or the center seat, I take the aisle seat and stretch my legs while he sits cramped in the middle. I'll let a man fight his way through the crowd at the bar to get our drinks, and if the next day at the office I meet his secretary in the women's room, I'll smile and gossip a little with her to see if I can find out what his staff think of him.

Many people, including some women in the Movement, might disagree with this attitude. I can understand their point of view—that real equality means no little privileges for being female. Well, while I'm waiting for real equality to happen, I'm going to use those privileges. You can decide for yourself.

If you plan ahead and are well organized, it is much easier to cope with the problems of travel and with being in the minority as a female business traveler. In this respect I believe that many women do have a real advantage over men. If you've raised three kids and regularly planned and executed Thanksgivings, Christmases, and other large events, you have a great deal more experience than any man has at handling crises and organizing complicated events. Maybe you can't put the experience on your résumé, but you should realize that detailed planning is detailed planning, whether it's a five-course dinner for eighteen relatives, or a three-week, eight-city tour of the divisions. And making a quick series of decisions in a crisis, whether it's a child who's fallen out of a tree or the necessity of getting from Rochester to Denver when the airport's fogged in and the rental agencies are all out of cars, requires the same kind of cool thinking and confidence. Women have been doing what had to be done for millennia, and keeping the company in business may even seem minor compared to other of life's problems.

In the remaining chapters of this book, I will discuss in

detail the kinds of planning and organization that are required for various business-travel situations, with examples of how I do it and how others do it. Because of Murphy's Law, many of my subjects will be concerned with how to prevent problems and how to cope when they do happen.

2

Packing

If I had to choose The One Essential Rule of Travel, it would be this: *Never take anything you can't carry.* No matter what your mode of transportation, it is certain that sooner or later, if it's yours, you'll have to tote it. For air travel, I would take it one step further: *You have to be able to carry everything at once. If you can't, don't take it.*

It is possible to go anywhere, for any length of time, with just those personal belongings that you can carry, and to do it without real hardship. Note that I am concerned only with business travel. If you are vacationing with a companion who will be with you for the whole trip, it is certainly feasible to plan on taking more than you yourself can carry at once. If your companion is stronger than you, or has less to carry, he or she can help with yours; or one of you can stand guard over extras while the other makes trips to the check-in counter, hotel lobby, or whatever. On a business trip, however, even if you are traveling with colleagues, you should *not* count on their help in carrying your personal luggage. They might offer to help, and you might even accept, but you should not make yourself dependent on them.

There are two types of business trips that might be exceptions to this rule. One is if you must take business supplies, materials, sales samples, or other paraphernalia in addition to your personal belongings. The other is an extended trip through several dramatically different climates, for which you must have a variety of leisure outfits as well as business clothes.

For the first situation, there is an easy solution: send the materials ahead. Have them shipped by ground or air transport to the place where you are doing business or to your hotel. If you use air express, they might even go on the same plane with you, but you might have to make an extra trip to and from the airport for your business materials. Even so, you will not have the chore of trying to get everything through the airport check-in, and from the pick-up area afterward, all by yourself. It will be someone else's responsibility door-to-door, or until you call for it.

Allow for the possibility that what you ship might not get there on time. (Almost everything gets there sooner or later; the airlines are good at tracing lost or misrouted items. They should be, having had so much experience at it.) Copies of legal documents or other essential papers can be in your personal luggage or—if they are really critical—in your carry-on case. If the items being sent are visual aids for a speech or lecture, be prepared to give the talk without them if you must. If they are multiple copies of a single item, such as a sales brochure or a text for a course, carry one copy with you; in an emergency, you can almost always find a photocopying machine to make more.

For the second situation, a multiple-stop trip requiring a variety of outfits, there are two possible solutions. One is the same, to send some things ahead to an intermediate stop. The other is a little more complicated, but can be more fun if you have the time for it. Start with what you'll need for the first leg of the trip, say, your warmest outfits for Juneau. When you leave that place, either throw enough away to lighten your luggage or send the cold-weather clothes back home. Then, when you arrive in Honolulu, go out and buy yourself extra clothes for that climate.

I have used this technique several times on week-long trips to Paris, not to save on luggage space, but just for the fun of it. I left with enough clothes for only a day or two, and spent the first day in Paris on a glorious shopping spree, buying several new outfits. This approach can have an added benefit if you're overseas for any length of time: you will probably not be asked to pay customs duty on clothing that is obviously used, especially if it has laundry marks or dry cleaning tags. (I've never tried, but I suspect this trick will not work with diamond rings or fur coats.)

An aid I've noticed being used by flight attendants and

other frequent travelers is a roller attachment for moving heavy bags. Some suitcases come with small wheels built in. Another aid is a folding metal tote that combines wheels and a handle. You'll still have to pick it up for escalators and stairs, but the wheels can save a lot of effort on those endless airport corridors. (One of the corollaries to Murphy's Law seems to be that the less time you have, the farther away your gate is.)

A little later on, I'll give some hints about how to keep down luggage weight. Even if your suitcase doesn't seem very heavy when you start out, it gets heavier and heavier the farther you have to carry it.

Luggage

There are two types of travelers in the world, soft-sided-luggage people and hard-sided-luggage people. I've tried both types of suitcases and finally decided on hard-sided, but I can understand soft-sided people.

Soft-sided cases have some advantages. They are usually the lightest. They are expansible, so you always seem to be able to cram in one more item—at least, until the zipper gives out. Some are very inexpensive. You can treat such a case badly (or shrug it off when the airline treats it badly) and not be bothered; when it gets too beat-up looking, you just throw it away and buy a new one. Finally, they come in lots of different colors, patterns, and prints, making it easier to identify yours as it comes out on the airport carousel.

On the other hand, hard-sided cases are usually better looking and they stay that way longer. They offer better protection for the items inside, and clothes get less wrinkled in them. Furthermore, in a pinch they're much nicer to sit on.

John T. Molloy, in his *The Woman's Dress for Success Book* (Chicago: Follett, 1977), has some very specific advice for a businesswoman. "There is only one type of luggage any woman in America should carry. It is a matched set of canvas luggage with belting leather strapping." He goes on to say that belting *leather* luggage, the ideal for a male executive, would make you look like you were trying to imitate a man, which is a no-no. But "feminine" luggage in light colors or prints is out too, because it doesn't carry any clout.

Well, on the basis of Molloy's advice, I've done a lot of looking in luggage stores and in the luggage departments of department stores. There is not a very wide choice of canvas luggage belted with leather. What I've found is all very expensive; the smallest item, say, a carry-on bag, costs $50 or $60. I figured it would cost upwards of $400 to put together a basic matched set of three suitcases. I didn't like much of what I saw either. One line had the designer's initials all over it, which is not to my taste. The best-looking set was in a light-colored canvas, *not* Scotchgarded; it would begin to look terribly dirty and scuffed in about a week and would be impossible to get clean. So until I find something I like, and can nerve myself to spend that much money for suitcases, I'm sticking with my plain, dark-colored molded cases—the type you see in ads still looking OK after being run over by a bulldozer.

As an aside, if you haven't yet read Molloy's book, I recommend it. You may take exception to some of his advice on what a businesswoman should wear, but it's all very interesting.

While we're on the subject of suitcases, a word about name tags. The airlines insist on a name-and-address tag for any item that's checked. It's also a good idea to put your name and address on the inside of each one too, in case the outside tag gets ripped off. But *don't* use your home address. It makes it too easy for potential burglars or other types of deviants to find out where you live, knowing that you're not at home. The best solution, one that most women travelers I know use, is to fashion a tag from your business card. It gives your name and office address and phone, which is probably more practical for someone finding your bag, anyway; if you're not at home, the airline won't be able to get in touch with you, whereas your office knows how to locate you.

Incidentally, I hope that your secretary or anyone else answering the phone at your office does not give out information about you over the phone, such as the fact that you're away on a trip, or the name of your hotel. All staff should be instructed never to do this, no matter who the caller says he is. They can just say you're not available at the moment, take a message, and pass it on to you.

But back to the subject. If you haven't done much traveling yet and are shopping for luggage, I would recommend that you start with a medium-priced, brand-name line, either hard- or soft-sided, whichever appeals to you. You can always move up to a more expensive line later, when you have a better idea of what you need. As a starter set, I would recommend one carry-on bag, of a size that will fit under an airplane seat, and two larger ones—"two-suiter" size or thereabouts. The carry-on bag should have one or more outside pockets, which you'll find very useful. Don't buy a giant-sized suitcase unless you're an Olympic weightlifter. You won't be able to carry it comfortably when it's full.

To complete the set, you'll need a garment bag. I like the type that has a special catch at the top to lock around the coat hangers; it prevents items from slipping down into the bag and getting wrinkled. Some people prefer a garment bag that has an outside, zippered pocket. They use the pocket for shoes, dirty laundry, or miscellaneous items that won't fit in the suitcase.

Carry-On

The garment bag is important. It has two major advantages. One is that it keeps outer clothes from getting wrinkled. No matter how cleverly I pack dresses and suits, they always seem to come out of a suitcase with wrinkles or creases. Second, you can carry a garment bag onto a plane. I believe that, technically, you're not supposed to take more than one carry-on item, in addition to your handbag. In practice, I've never had an airline refuse to let me carry on both a garment bag and an under-seat bag. (On many trips, I've had four items: attaché case, handbag, under-seat case, and garment bag.) Many planes have places to hang the garment bag, and some have stowage areas for your case too. Or, the garment bag—being soft—can be stowed in the overhead rack. It won't crush anyone's head if it happens to fall out during turbulence.

The garment bag plus the under-seat case is the secret of being able to go anywhere for any length of time with only carry-on luggage. You can easily get four or five dresses or suits in the garment bag, and everything else in the suitcase. Five different outfits are more than enough. By "mixing and matching," as the fashion mags say, you can switch them around often enough to keep from getting too bored or appearing too often in the same outfit. For a very long trip (which I would define as more than six weeks), I would take one or two things that had only a short time left in their useful life, then throw them away after a few wearings and buy something new.

On short trips, one or two nights away, I often take just the garment bag. Outer clothes go in the bag, and underwear goes in the zippered pocket. In my briefcase I put my toilet articles and miscellaneous items like jewelry or an extra pair of shoes. This is one reason I prefer a briefcase with a top zipper and a side pocket to an attaché case. You can put personal stuff in the bottom and business papers over them, and carry things like your plane ticket in the pocket where they're always handy. If the briefcase isn't too full, I put my handbag in the top.

This has been a help on several occasions when the ticket agent was eyeing all my carry-on stuff; by definition, if you take your plane ticket out of it, it's a handbag and doesn't count as carry-on luggage.

My handbag is always a shoulder bag, so if necessary I can carry it separately over my shoulder and still have two hands free. The garment bag can go over your arm, and you *still* have two hands free.

But when you're carrying everything onto the plane, weight becomes important. In some airports, you'll be walking for what seems like miles, and if it wasn't heavy when you started out, it soon is. I go to great lengths to cut down on the weight in these situations.

Personal items that weigh the most are shoes, bottles, and appliances like hair dryers. Keep these to a minimum.

For a short trip, I try to take only one pair of shoes, being sure they'll look OK with any evening outfit I might take. And I'm wearing the shoes, so they don't need to be carried. Only *in extremis* will I wear or carry boots. If you're going from airport to bus to hotel, you probably don't need boots anyway, even in the worst winter weather.

Plastic bottles are essential for travel, of course. Many cosmetics and toilet items are sold in plastic. If you have anything in a glass bottle, transfer it. If you've ever had a bottle of shampoo break in your suitcase, you've learned this lesson the hard way. Sample sizes are a great convenience too.

Think twice about any appliance that's heavy. Do you

really need an iron, even a "travel" one? I gave up toting mine long ago, and have never missed it. You have three alternatives, in descending order of convenience and effectiveness: send things out to the hotel valet service for pressing; call housekeeping and ask to borrow the hotel's iron and ironing board; or hang the wrinkled items in the bathroom, turn on the hot water in the shower full blast, and close the door and go away for fifteen minutes.

That last technique is known to all travelers, and it usually works fine. The only time it backfired on me was in an older hotel; after ten minutes I heard the most awful crashing sounds, and opened the bathroom door to see, through the steam, that half the tiles had fallen off the wall and smashed on the floor. I figured that would have happened soon anyway if the tiles were that loose, and when the steam cleared I called the front desk to report, in indignation, how the walls had fallen while I had the shower on. I didn't mention that I wasn't there at the time.

If you wash your hair the night before, it'll dry by itself and you don't need a hair dryer. I do compromise and take a curling iron for touch-ups.

As you pack, think about whether you *really* need that item. An umbrella? What's the weather forecast for the city you're visiting? How much will you be out of doors, anyway? Maybe a scarf would do. Business papers too. Do you really need all that? I stopped toting blank pads of paper when it dawned on me that *every* office has pads, I could always get one by asking.

I cut the weight of my belongings down so far that one

day, just before a plane trip, I realized I was paying for things with pennies so as to have fewer coins in my wallet. That's taking the idea a little bit too far, I think.

Flying with only carry-on luggage has three important advantages. The first two are obvious. If you carry it with you, the airlines can't lose or misroute it. And you save time by not having to wait for the plane to be unloaded.

The third advantage applies especially in business travel. By having only carry-on bags, you have more flexibility to change your travel plans at midpoint. Let's say that you're flying from Cincinnati to San Francisco, with a connection in Denver. You arrive in Denver and discover that your connecting flight, which originated in Houston, has been delayed. You find, however, that another airline has a flight leaving for San Francisco in ten minutes. If you'd checked your luggage through to San Francisco from Cincinnati, you'd be stuck—not even enough time to call the first airline and try to get your things transferred. With only carry-on stuff, you can get your ticket changed on the spot and be on your way at once, arriving in San Francisco on time. It can save hours of waiting around in airports, and get you to your destination on time more often.

Playing the airline game this way is discussed in more detail in the chapter on air travel.

Driving

None of the above applies if you are using your own car for the trip. Your only limit is what will fit in the trunk. If you must, use the back seat too, but put there the things you would least mind losing if someone broke into the car. I would suggest, however, that you use the same "Can I carry it?" test for packing the car. You can make as many trips as necessary from car to motel room, but each single item should be manageable enough for you to handle by yourself if you have to.

One man I know packs everything in a trunk that just fills the trunk of his car. It has lift-out compartments. He can get everything into the trunk and doesn't need to fold his suits. It's very neat and well-organized. He swings the trunk onto his shoulder and has everything into the hotel room and unpacked in a matter of minutes. I wish I could do it. He's six feet four and used to play semipro football.

Just about everyone I know who travels often by car considers music to be important. I have an eight-track tape player installed in my car, and a boxful of tapes of my favorite music. I also have a portable eight-track stereo player, so I can transfer the box of tapes from car to hotel room and have some good music. Combination AM-FM stereo tape players are popular too for hotel-room use. One auditor I know takes this idea to its limit by carrying around a full-sized stereo system, complete with separate speakers and a rack of LP's. I don't know what his neighbors in the hotel think of it, but he has some super little parties in his room. Another man, also an auditor, has a cassette tape of his dog barking, to play when he gets homesick. (Are all auditors weird, or just the ones I know?)

The point is, that with a car you can indulge yourself. Take a complete wardrobe if you want. Iron *and* ironing board. Several women I know travel with portable sewing machines and use their free evenings and weekends making clothes for themselves and presents for friends. I usually have a bag of embroidery or an afghan I'm crocheting to work on while watching television. I suppose you could even take your teddy bear collection, if you felt the need.

Planning What to Take

Every magazine article I've ever seen on Getting Ready for Your Vacation has a list of items to take, right down to the bottle of aspirin and miniature manicure kit. Some even have illustrations of planned wardrobes. You know, the striped shirt that will go with *either* the blue pants *or* the wrap-around skirt.

Nuts.

Pack the things that you *know* you're going to need, like toothpaste and underwear, and then, if you feel like carrying that much, add things that are not essential but would make you feel better, such as your wigs or your bath oil; and then if you think you still have room for them, add things you might need if something went wrong, like a first-aid kit or an electric handwarmer; and finally, put in things it would be good to have if something unexpectedly nice happened—maybe your golf clubs, your diaphragm, your most gorgeous disco dress, or your three-bottle portable bar kit, depending on what your pleasures are.

Keep in mind that if you forget something essential, or if something you never thought you'd need *becomes* essential, you'll probably be able to buy it. In this way I have acquired several evening purses, an extra contact lens (left eye), various cold remedies, and untold combs, nail files, panty hose, and safety pins. Don't be like the tourist arriving in London, who got off the plane and wailed, "I forgot my toothbrush! What *am* I going to do???" Buy one, dammit. The rest of the world is not composed of unwashed savages; they *have* heard of tampons in Kansas City and laxatives in Madrid.

I used to make extensive lists of things, to ensure I wouldn't forget anything. I still forgot things. Everyone seems to specialize in forgetting something in particular. For me, it's shower caps and belts. I can *never* remember to pack that shower cap, unless I have thoughtfully put it over the knob of the front door so I encounter it as I'm leaving the house. Other people have trouble with their alarm clock or their hand cream. Once, I forgot an entire suitcase, all packed and ready to go—and didn't even notice I was without it until I got to the hotel in Milan.

I don't make lists anymore because it's too time-consuming. I figure that if I'm going to forget it, I'd forget to put it on the list too. But I do start thinking about what I want to take a few days ahead of time, so that I'm sure to have the laundry done and the things I want back from the dry cleaners.

Clothes. For business, take what you'd wear to the

office at home. Maybe your best outfits but not strikingly different ones. Business dress is just about the same everywhere. You might make a few adjustments for local conditions. If you think the natives are more conservative in the city you're visiting, leave the pantsuits at home and take only dresses and skirted suits. Put in an evening outfit if you know there's going to be an occasion to wear it. Take warmer or lighter clothes if the climate is going to be different. If you don't know these things, ask someone who's been there, or call up and ask the people *there*, or consult a guidebook.

A few more words on the subject of evening outfits. I have found that on a business trip, something "dressy" for evening is rarely essential. Businessmen wear the same suit and shirt they had on all day at the office. You can do the same. This is true even at conventions and conferences, where there is often a special dinner one evening. Wives accompanying their businessmen husbands are the ones who dress up in long gowns. The businesswomen wear the same type of suit they wore all day. There seems to be some kind of mystique about this, as if the suit were a uniform. I usually conform, but sometimes I don't. If I feel like it, or want to make the occasion a little festive, I'll take a cocktail dress or disco-style jump suit. Other times, I just don't bother.

If you really want to get into the subject of what to wear, read the book by Molloy mentioned earlier in this chapter. If you follow his advice to the letter, you could have half a dozen different wardrobes for different cities and different situations. For example, he says that Detroit is the only city where a brown suit is the best choice, and tells you what to wear if you're a *non-black* saleswoman calling on black buyers, and what to wear if you're a *black* saleswoman calling on . . . well, it gets kind of complicated, read it for yourself.

For cosmetics and other toiletries, some superwomen claim that they always keep a toilet kit stocked with everything they need, and just pop it in a suitcase. I'm not that well organized. I do keep a toilet kit just for travel, and keep things in it. For example, if I see a small sample-sized bottle of shampoo or moisturizer I like at the drugstore, I'll buy it and put it in the kit. When there's only a few days' worth of toothpaste left in the tube, that goes in the kit too.

I rarely forget essential toilet items. Here's how to make sure you don't either. The night before the day you're leaving, take out the toilet kit and check what's in it. Then, as you do your nightly routine, and again getting ready in the morning, look at everything you use. Don't put it down without checking whether it should go in the kit. Deodorant? Toothbrush? Eye drops? Cosmetics? Consider each item in your hand and decide if it goes in the kit or back on the shelf. Any item that you don't use either the night before or in the morning is not an essential.

If you're really hopeless, start three days ahead and make lists. Don't close any suitcase until everything on every list is crossed out. Otherwise, you'll open the same suitcase five times to double-check five different items. When you're as sure as you can be that nothing's missing, close everything up, mentally say to hell with it, and go.

Finally, here's a general rule to keep in mind when you're deciding what, and how much, to take. It's in the same category as the principle explained in the first chapter, that the number of miles is irrelevant, it's how long it takes to get there that counts. This rule is, *It's not where you're going that counts, it's how long you're going to be there.* Some people plan and pack as if a week on the opposite coast were ten times as complicated as a week in a city a hundred miles away. Nonsense. Don't go to all that trouble. Three days in London is exactly the same as three days in New York or Los Angeles or Broken Bow, Nebraska. Three days is three days. Pack accordingly.

How to Pack

At this point, I was going to give some very complicated instructions for folding and packing. One system, for example, has you folding things over each other in layers, something like the way pop-up tissues are packed in a box. But it all seems like so much trouble, and I'm sure that the first time I opened the suitcase I'd ruin it all anyway.

Besides, you don't need to bother folding if you've got a garment bag. Outer clothing goes in that and will arrive reasonably free of wrinkles.

Most of the best hints for packing are just plain common sense. If you'd like a review of them, here they are:

- Airline regulations forbid combustible, noxious, or otherwise hazardous materials. Don't take lighter fluid, hand grenades, or your .44 Magnum. Also, if you are entering California by road, your car will be inspected for vegetable matter—fruit, plants, and the like—to protect the agriculture business from accidental importation of pests.
- Put hair spray, shampoo, and other spillables or breakables in plastic bags. Put shoes in plastic bags too, to protect your other things.
- Put small items inside of shoes.
- Roll soft things like nightgowns and sweaters.
- Fold outer clothing along seam lines.
- Pack heavy items, like shoes, on the side of the case opposite the handle. If you put them near the handle, when you pick up the case they'll slide down and crush everything else.
- If you must pack a fragile item, put it as near the center as possible, and surround it firmly with soft clothing.
- Leave small items like gloves and scarves for last and tuck them into corners.
- Be sure your alarm clock isn't set to ring.
- Pack so the weight is evenly distributed from side to side. Otherwise you'll be lurching along out of balance.

Remember that all luggage is subject to inspection by the airlines. Carry-on items, *including* your handbag, go through the X-ray machine at the airport. It is claimed that the machine won't hurt film, but if you have your camera in your hand and ask that it not be X-rayed, they'll oblige and just inspect it visually. I sometimes travel with video tapes and computer media, like disk packs, and I ask that these not be X-rayed either. I don't know that any damage would be done, but I'd rather not take the chance.

If something looks suspicious in the machine, you may be asked to let them open the bag. Sometimes my curling rod seems to get the attention of the security people. They are very discreet in their poking around, but still, I pack dirty underwear so it's not right on top and visible to all. If you are carrying a stash, or other items you don't want to call attention to, remember this.

The only time I was ever really embarrassed by a security check was when, for some reason that is now lost to me, I had been in a novelty store and bought one of those joke gadgets that issue an insane laugh when you push the button. The security guard reached for it and set it off before I could stop her. Everyone within half a mile was riveted to the spot, and I wanted to disappear under the table.

Security checks in European airports are often much more rigorous than in the United States, especially on airlines like El Al and in countries that have experienced terrorist attacks. In these situations be prepared for a full body search. Passengers rarely object—it would be foolish to do so. In fact, I get nervous if the check doesn't seem thorough enough. The more careful they are, the better I feel.

Now, a few words about what to pack in which case. If you're not carrying on everything, decide what you want to check through before you start packing. Try to put everything you need for twenty-four hours of life in your carry-on bag. This would include most of your cosmetics and other toilet items and a change of underwear. Also put anything valuable, such as your jewelry and camera, in the carry-on bag.

If you're driving and will be stopping overnight on the road, pack everything you need for the stop in one bag. This will save you from having to take everything into the hotel. The English have a system for long sea voyages that I admire and emulate. Each case is marked WOV (Wanted on Voyage) or NWOV (Not Wanted on Voyage). Divide your belongings up into WOV and NWOV categories for packing, and put the NWOV cases into the car first.

Now that everything's packed, there's one last subject. That is whether or not to lock your suitcases. My theory is that it is useless to lock anything. If someone wants to get into your bag, the lock is not going to stop them for more than thirty seconds, and you'll get the bag back (if at all) ruined. Furthermore, I think that if a bag is locked, a potential thief is going to be much more interested, assuming that you wouldn't have bothered if there was nothing valuable in it. Anything I'd really hate to lose is with me in my carry-on luggage, or if I'm driving it goes with me into my room. I've never locked a checked case, and never had anything stolen from one. You can decide for yourself.

Clothes for the Journey

What to wear on the plane, or while driving, depends on two things. One is where you'll be just before departing, and the other is where you'll be immediately upon arriving. If either one of those is a business setting, you'll be wearing business clothes.

For example, in my present job I make frequent short trips, of one or two days, by air. I often leave from the office in the late afternoon, to arrive at my destination in time for dinner and a night's sleep, so I can be at the office first thing in the morning. I'll be wearing a business suit for the trip, because that's what I wore to the office that day. Or, I'll leave first thing in the morning to arrive at the office I'm visiting before lunch. Same thing— I dress for the office.

At other times, though, I may be leaving from home and heading for the hotel on arrival. This happens if I need to be at my destination first thing Monday morning —I travel on Sunday evening. Sometimes I want to spend the weekend in the city I'm visiting, to see old friends (or a new one) or relatives. Those times, I travel on Friday night or Saturday.

If I'm not coming from, or going directly to, a business situation, I dress strictly for comfort. That means jeans, a T-shirt, and sandals in warm weather, or jeans, a sweater, and maybe short boots in the winter. Some people would differ with me on this. They feel that on a business trip, you should always be dressed for business. I figure that after five and before nine, it's my time and I'll wear my clothes and be comfortable, and not have to worry about spilling the coffee if the plane hits rough weather. If flight attendants and hotel clerks are unimpressed with my appearance, too bad.

Only once have I got caught on this. I was traveling from Columbus, Ohio, to Chicago on a Sunday evening and planned to get to my hotel fairly early. At O'Hare, I met a group of businessmen from my company, men I knew and had worked with; they were on their way from Detroit to San Francisco and were stopping over in Chicago for dinner. They were dressed fit to kill—three-piece suits, wing-tip shoes, sincere ties, and the rest. They took in my paint-stained blue jeans and the T-shirt that said "Evil Woman" on it and gulped a few times. One finally stammered out that they were planning to go to dinner and would love to have me join them. I excused myself and went into the nearest women's room with my suitcase. I emerged ten minutes later in high-heeled sandals, slinky black pants, and a green silk shirt with my grandmother's cameo pinned to it. They all beamed, and we had an excellent dinner.

About that spilled coffee. If you're wearing business clothes for the trip, it's best to choose dark colors and spongeable fabrics. Almost any disaster can then be mopped or dabbed at until you look reasonably presentable again.

I suppose I should say something about shoes too, although I no longer buy shoes that aren't comfortable for walking. Shoes with very high heels, platform soles, or other features that make it difficult to walk or stand for long periods are dreadful on a trip. On planes, many people find that their feet swell. I've seen women getting off a plane barefoot because they took their shoes off and couldn't get them back on again. Wear your plainest, most comfortable shoes for the journey. Sneakers are absolutely tops. Next best are low-heeled pumps, or—with pants—short boots, also low-heeled. And, of course, never wear new shoes on a trip.

All of the above applies to automobile journeys as well as plane trips. Whenever possible, wear clothes that can withstand spilled coffee and shoes that feel good for driving. Being comfortable has an added benefit, if it means fewer distractions and therefore a happier and more alert driver. Nothing is more important than safety when you're driving.

3

Getting There— on the Road

It was 3 A.M. on a cool summer morning. I was somewhere in the middle of Oregon, sitting in my car while it warmed up a little. I was on my way from San Francisco to Seattle. I had stopped late in the afternoon the day before, had a nice swim in the motel's pool, dinner, and an early bedtime. I was ready to start driving again, and I looked in the rear-view mirror, I saw a trail of little footprints right up the middle of the rear window. Some small animal, I think a raccoon, had been investigating my car in the night.

In the thousands of miles I've driven in North America in the last few years, there have been many such incidents that have become treasured memories. Some are much more dramatic, such as the first view of Salt Lake City as I came down out of the Rockies, or the blazing foliage of New England in October. And then there was the double rainbow in the hills of northern Washington State, crop-dusting in Southern California, following the trail of the Donner party and seeing ruts left by wagon trains, the spectacular scenery of the Sierra Nevada mountains.

These are all things that air travelers can't experience. True, there are many disadvantages to surface travel, not the least of which is the time it takes. But for those who can, or must, travel by road, there are compensations. In this chapter, I'll relate some of my experiences and try to give a distillation of what I have learned. Even travelers who usually go by air often have reason to use local roads both in cities and in rural areas (including business travelers in rental cars), so this information may be helpful for them too.

Choice of Vehicle

Buying a car is a very personal decision, with many variables to take into account. I am not, therefore, about to recommend any particular make of car. I will say that if I were buying a new car today for heavy freeway travel, I would get the largest one I could afford. The primary reason for that choice is comfort. It's much easier to do 500 miles a day in a large, easy-handling car than it is in a budget subcompact. Even large cars today are getting much better gas mileage than they used to, and today's "big" car is smaller than it was eight or ten years ago.

I would also seriously consider a diesel-powered engine, for reasons of economy and environment. I think that the manufacturers will be offering more and more diesel cars to choose from in the next few years. If you're traveling mainly between cities via the freeways, there's no worry at all about being able to get fuel.

On the other hand, some of you may need to travel to relatively remote areas, in bad weather, over rough terrain. This presents a different kind of problem. Perhaps a four-wheel-drive vehicle might be the best choice in such a situation.

If you travel by air and have to leave your car at the airport for long periods of time, you'll probably think twice about a big, new car. I know several people who have gone out and bought a second car just for this purpose, an old clunker or beat-up pick-up truck that they don't have to worry about while they're away.

John T. Molloy, the *Dress for Success* guru I've mentioned before, recommends that for image purposes a woman should have a classy but not overly large car. (It seems a car is a wardrobe accessory.) He mentions the Mercedes specifically, arguing that a very large car overwhelms a woman and makes her look less important in comparison.

One nice way to shop around for a new car is by using the rental car agency. Every time I need to rent a car, which is often, I ask what the choice is and pick one I haven't driven before. You may quickly learn of certain cars you *don't* want to buy, and you'll get an idea of how useful the various options are. Just take a minute to look over the controls before you drive off. They're putting the headlight dimmer switch in the darndest places these days. I had a new Thunderbird recently, and when I got to our plant I couldn't get the key out of the ignition. It took a phone call to Hertz on their emergency number to find out that you have to push a secret button on the opposite side of the steering column in order to release the key. I'm still trying to figure out the rationale for that. The only thing I can think of is that it would be handy if a would-be thief jumped into the car from the passenger side and tried to grab the key out of the ignition. If he wants it that bad, though, my opinion is to let him have it. And anyway, why not just keep the doors locked?

Options and Accessories

Comfort is not unrelated to safety, of course. If you get cramped and tired in your car, you're not in the best possible safety situation. You may not be able to go out and buy a new car for long-distance business travel, but you can add some features to the ones you have, or keep them in mind for when you start thinking about trading in.

The first thing on my list is good rubber. Even if you couldn't afford anything else, I'd recommend spending money for the best tires. To me, this means steel-belted radials. Nothing beats them. I drove all last winter on steel-belted radials, from Wisconsin to Georgia to Vermont, and couldn't have been more pleased with them. On inspecting the tires a few months ago, I found that I'd picked up not just one, but two big nails in the left front tire. Either nail would have meant a blow-out with conventional tires, but I didn't even know I had them until I saw them. The tire hadn't even lost any air. It can't be repaired, but it's perfectly serviceable as my spare tire until I need to buy new ones. I've got 35,000 miles on these, and they're probably good for next winter too.

Air conditioning is number two. It's essential in some parts of the country, and almost essential everywhere else in warm weather. It adds enormously to your comfort and therefore to safety. You arrive looking good, not sweaty and rumpled. And it adds to the trade-in value of your car.

The next item is seat belts. Every car has them now, of course, so what can I say except *use them*. I believe the statistics. Seat belts save lives. Some women complain that they're uncomfortable with a seat belt. I've come close to ruining one of my best friendships with a woman who doesn't like to use the seat belt when she's a passenger in my car, or when driving her own. I feel so strongly about this that it's got to the point where we just don't travel in the same car, in order to forestall the inevitable argument. I use mine so automatically that I feel very uncomfortable without it. I even feel uncomfortable on planes when I first fasten the lap belt—it doesn't feel right without the shoulder part. Use your seat belt.

Another benefit of the seat belt is that it helps you to

be a better driver. You don't sway as much going around corners and curves, so you're able to keep better control of the car.

I consider a radio to be essential too. It helps keep you awake, and can inform you of potentially hazardous weather and road situations. I think a stereo system is a good investment in this respect—the better the sound, the more apt you are to use it. The same for FM. One feature I don't have in my car, but wish I had, is the foot-operated station finder. It automatically seeks out the next signal, saving you a lot of dial-twiddling to find the local station when you're in an unfamiliar area. And I've already mentioned my tape deck, which gives me some keep-awake, sing-along music when there's nothing particularly good on the radio.

I've driven cars with tilt-type steering wheels, cruise control, and other expensive options. They're very nice to have if you can afford them.

CB radios are beginning to pass from fad status to being standard options. I like to have a CB for long-distance driving, but I must admit I don't use mine much around the city. It can be very comforting to have on long trips, and good company at night. You get a different kind of picture of what's going on out there by listening to the truck drivers' chatter. It can contribute to safety too, because you may hear of an accident ahead and be able to slow down sooner, or get weather reports for the road ahead. And, of course, other drivers will inform you of where the "Smokies," the police, are waiting. I am not recommending that you use the CB to enable you to exceed the speed limit with impunity. Anyway, if you really want to play that game, you'll need a fuzz-buster—a radar detector—too. I'm not an expert in this subject, so I will say no more.

If you don't have a CB and are planning to install one, I'd offer the following advice. First, get one of the many popular books on the subject to learn a little about the jargon used on CB. Be careful in picking your handle—any woman with a handle that is even slightly suggestive or open to misinterpretation may find herself in difficulty. (Unless, of course, you're on the road with your CB because you're a prostitute, in which case I'll assume you know what you're doing and don't need any advice from me.)

My second piece of advice would be to use the CB mostly to listen. You don't have to reply to other drivers who see you and ask you to answer. But if you feel comfortable doing so, you can have some interesting conversations. Just remember the one essential rule of CB: never give your real name or your home address. If you really want to meet someone you've been talking to, arrange a rendezvous at a stop you know will be well-lighted and populated, such as a service area restaurant.

And finally, in choosing your equipment, get the cheapest possible set and aerial. Prices are coming down all the time; I paid about sixty dollars for mine, including aerial and installation. Insurance premiums for CB's are very high, so with a cheap set you'll feel less sorry when it is ripped off, which sooner or later will happen.

Later on in this chapter, I'll discuss handling emergency breakdowns, including using the CB to get help.

Driving Skills

I wish it were possible to take an advanced driving course, or for ordinary citizens to be able to sign up for practice and instruction of the type given to police officers. There is such a course in England, given by their equivalent of the AAA. It's tough, and if you pass the tests, you automatically get lower insurance premiums, among other benefits. As it is, most of us don't even know it if we've picked up bad habits or could improve our skills.

In spite of all those sexist jokes about woman drivers, women are better drivers than men, and this is reflected in lower insurance premiums. The reason usually offered for this is that women are less aggressive. On the other hand, I think that in some ways a car is like a gun. It's an equalizer. You have just as much power and potential destructive ability when you're driving as a man twice your size—provided his car isn't bigger or tougher than yours. But it is nice to know that the statistics are on your side, that you're less likely to have an accident.

There are a lot of things that are never taught in driving school. I've found that the best way to improve my driving is to read books about driving and then practice the recommended techniques. Another way is to ask an experienced driver, one whose car you've been in and whose skill you admire, to give you some pointers.

That was how I learned to drive in heavy snow conditions. It was during the first winter I spent in New England as an adult. I asked a cousin who had lived there all her life. She took me out to a very large, very empty parking lot and let me practice accelerating, braking, and cornering on the packed snow. I'd recommend exactly the same kind of practice session for any of you who aren't used to winter driving and must head north for business trips. It's a scary feeling the first time the car just slides away and you have no control at all. With a little practice, you learn at what speeds you can take various types of curves safely, how to steer *into* the skid, and to keep your foot off that brake no matter what. It's also comforting to know that at 20 mph, with your seat belt fastened, you're unlikely to be seriously injured no matter what you hit.

The first rule for driving in bad weather is *don't*. I was on my way from Chicago to Atlanta during that dreadful winter of 1977–78, trying without success to keep ahead of a storm. The third time I saw a car ahead of me spin out of control and end up on the median strip, I decided that no job was worth that. Besides, at 30 mph it was going to take me a week to get to Atlanta. I left the freeway at the next exit and went right to the nearest motel. As I pulled up to the front entrance I realized that my options were no longer open. The driveway into the motel was all downhill and solid ice, and short of hiring a team of horses there was no way I was ever going to get the car back up the driveway until it had been cleared. This was in Kentucky, where the nearest snowplow was probably fifty miles away and stuck in a drift. As it turned out, I was there for three days before some bright individual got some sand to spread on the driveway.

In the worst conditions you're not safe no matter how slowly you're going. I learned this during that same winter, on the Ohio Turnpike. The road was clear and dry when I started, but then it began to rain and as dusk fell so did the temperature. In a matter of minutes I was driving not on a wet pavement but on sheer ice. So was everyone else. The big trucks couldn't make it up the hills. It's really frightening to be stopped dead still and suddenly realize your car is sliding backwards. Each time traffic halted, the warmth of the tires would melt the ice a little and cars would just slide. Again, I got off at the next exit and stopped for the night. It took three hours to drive the thirty miles to the exit.

Here are some examples of things I've learned from books that make sense and seem to work in practice:

- If you're being tailgated in heavy, fast-moving traffic, *slow down* to increase the distance between you and the car ahead. If the idiot behind you rear-ends you, you're less likely to hit the car ahead and start a chain accident.

- I needed new windshield-wiper blades, or so I thought. But the new ones didn't improve matters at all, I was still peering through streaks whenever it rained. Then I read somewhere that the wax used in automatic carwashes can build up on the windshield and cause streaking. Sure enough, a good scrub with glass cleaner cured the problem. Now why couldn't

I have thought of that myself? Maybe everybody else in the world knows it already.

- Keep either your left arm or your left leg in contact with the side of the car. This gives you a better "feel" for the road and the way the car is performing.

One thing that doesn't help me in books or magazine articles on driving is descriptions of various noises the engine can make and what problems they signal. I wish someone would put out a tape or an LP record with real sounds of knocks, skips, whee-whirrs, and clunk-clunks so I'd have something to compare with.

The most valuable advice I ever got from a book was on left-foot braking. It works only with an automatic transmission, of course. Because I learned to drive with standard transmission, I always felt uneasy with an automatic because my left foot had nothing to do. So I started left-foot braking. The idea is that you keep your left foot near or poised over the brake pedal at all times. The advantages are faster braking in emergency situations and smoother driving. The major disadvantage is that if you're not doing it right you'll rest your foot on the pedal and wear out your brakes much faster. Also, it can be awkward at night if you need your left foot for the headlight dimmer. I've found, though, that on those few occasions when I'm driving at night on an untraveled road, I have no trouble going back to right-foot braking to keep my left foot free for the dimmer.

If that extra fraction of a second of braking time one

day saved a child's life, it would be more than worth the effort of learning the technique.

Car Maintenance

Take care of your car maintenance yourself. Leaving it up to a husband, brother, or other male relative is not only not very liberated, it can cause you no end of difficulty. You need to know what has been done to the car at each servicing, and at least be able to ask intelligent questions of the mechanic.

Read your owner's manual and use the servicing checklists. If the car was bought second-hand and doesn't have a manual, you can get one by writing to the manufacturer; be sure to specify the year and model of your car. Failing this, there are now a number of good books for women about cars, and most of these have a checklist of what should be done at each servicing.

In my family, the boys often were outdoors with their heads under the hood of the pick-up truck that wouldn't run, receiving a running commentary from uncle or grandfather about the innards of the engine. The girls (including me) were in the kitchen being taught that you bring the water to a boil before you add the spaghetti, and always put oregano in the sauce. Both are valuable skills, but I wish I had been encouraged to go out and look at what was wrong with the pick-up once in a while. I always defend women who do something stupid to their cars. We're not *born* knowing how to change a flat tire or that there are two different fan belts (three, if you have air conditioning).

If you can find one, take a course on auto mechanics. The "Y" in some big cities offers such a course. Or, read up on the subject. You will learn most, however, by taking responsibility for the car yourself. If you have a local mechanic who is not only honest and reliable, but who will tell you what he did to the car and show you worn parts, cherish him. Take advantage of his friendliness to ask questions, no matter how dumb they may sound at first. But don't expect a crash course in auto mechanics in exchange for an oil and lube; he's busy and lost time may be reflected in the labor charges on your bill. Ask one or two pertinent questions each time. Also, other men are usually only too pleased to show off their expertise. Ask in the office, "My mechanic says I'm going to need new shocks soon. How do I tell if he's right?" and you'll get a free dissertation on the care and feeding of shock absorbers.

My car developed a squeak in the power steering last week. I looked up "power steering" in the owner's manual, and it said you have to change the fluid once in a while. I drove over to the service station and asked the man to check it. He showed me where to look, but said the fluid was fine and the problem was probably a dry fan belt. He showed me the fan belts, also pointing out how to tell if they're getting worn, and squirted the offender with some silicone lubrication. Now I know something about power steering and fan belts.

When I'm traveling, I always take my car to a company dealer for servicing. There's no guarantee that they're more honest than the people at the service station on the corner, but at least I have the assurance that the mechanics there know something about my type of car. (I always get nervous when a mechanic can't find the hood release.) Also—and this happened to one of the people I work with—if you get 300 miles down the road and the engine bursts into flames because they left a rag inside, you can go to the nearest dealer to complain. In case of gross negligence, you can take your complaint to the zone office or even higher, even if you are never going to be back in the town where the work was originally done.

Read your owner's manual to find out how often to change the engine oil and how often to have a tune-up. Tune-ups are done at less frequent intervals than oil changes. If you're on a tight budget and don't care about the resale or trade-in value of the car, stick to the schedule in the manual. Otherwise, have the oil changed more often. My manual recommends an oil change every 7,000 miles, but I have it done at 4,000. Also, the manual recommends changing the oil filter with every other oil change, but I have it done every time. There is up to a quart of old oil in the filter, and it goes into circulation again with the new oil unless you change the filter too. I know one person with a new Lincoln who changes the oil every 2,000 miles. The more often you change it, the better it is for the engine.

I had a tune-up and oil change last winter at a dealer in Wisconsin, just before starting on the trip to Atlanta.

Halfway there, on the freeway, the engine just stopped. It started again right away, but the same thing happened five miles later. I got to the nearest service station, which, luckily, had an honest mechanic. He diagnosed the problem as a clogged gas filter, and changed it on the spot. Cost: $2. That filter should have been changed with the tune-up. The moral of this is, read your owner's manual and make a list of what should be checked each time you take the car in. Don't rely on the mechanic to do everything that should be done. Don't rely on *anybody* else. Your life depends on that car, and you are responsible.

It is a good idea, too, to keep a log. Every time some work is done, write down the date, the mileage on the odometer, and what was done. You can also note gas purchases to calculate how many miles to the gallon you are getting. The log can be very useful if you are on the road and a mechanic says, "It's probably time to rotate the tires. When did you last have it done?" You can save yourself some unnecessary service charges. The log will be useful, too, if you ever want to sell the car. It will prove that you have changed the oil often and have otherwise kept the engine in good condition.

Freeway Driving

Long-distance business travel means freeways. If you're on vacation and have lots of time, it is nice to get off onto the back roads and see the country. That's not our main concern here, though. America's freeway system really is excellent, as anyone who has tried to make good time on long-distance trips in other parts of the world will tell you. In spite of the damage done by the bad winters of the mid-seventies, our freeways are still the best roads in the world. And, except at rush hours around big cities, they are still relatively uncrowded. The planners' forecasts of peak traffic loads, made when the system was being planned, have never been realized, due mostly to the oil crisis and the rising cost of gas.

To take advantage of these good roads and to get where you're going in a reasonable amount of time, you can't dawdle. That doesn't mean you should speed, however. In almost all parts of the country I have found that with good road conditions, the flow of traffic tends to be around 60 mph, five miles over the "double-nickle" limit. I've never heard of anyone who got a ticket for 60—that extra five seems to be a grace margin. There are a few places where the local police have a reputation for being extraordinarily tough, so if you find that the flow of traffic seems to have suddenly slowed a little, do the same. Your CB, if you have one, will probably inform you of where these spots are.

Some states have a reputation for allowing even faster speeds. At the time I was in Georgia, for example, I was told that by state law you couldn't get a ticket for doing 60, and 65 was OK. It was still illegal, but no tickets. And Michigan, perhaps because it is the home of the big auto companies, has a reputation for ignoring the 55-mph limit; maybe they like to pretend that the oil crisis never happened. I don't recommend testing this, however. As with seat belts, I believe the statistics. The 55-mph limit has saved many lives.

As a general rule, you are safest and will feel most comfortable going at the same speed as the general flow of traffic. If that speed seems to me to be too high, I just get over on the inside lane and keep steady at between 55 and 60. Anyone who wants to can pass, that's fine with me. If the general flow is slower, I don't try to push it, but slow down like everyone else.

The difference between 55 and 60, or 60 and 65, is not very great anyway if you work it out. What *will* slow you down are frequent or lengthy stops. At 60, thirty minutes is thirty miles. If you're trying to make fast time and get there, keep driving. Stop only as often as necessary for safety. For most people, that means about ten minutes every two hours for the first eight hours of driving. Get out, stretch, walk around, go to the bathroom, get a cup of coffee.

If you have another driver to share with, you can probably do a little better than that. You might stop, say, only once every three hours for the same routine, and change drivers then.

Most people I have talked to consider that eight to ten hours per day is a safe driving limit for one person. I have heard many stories about drivers who have done twenty or thirty hours at a stretch, sometimes with the help of drugs. This is definitely not for me, nor for you, I hope. Nothing could be that important, to justify risking your life and the lives of others.

It is possible, even if you're not particularly tired, to

get "hypnotized" by the long stretches of highway. This seems to happen mostly at night, when there's no scenery to look at. Truck drivers call it white-line fever. To avoid that risk, use your radio, your tape deck, and your CB for entertainment. Be aware of the temperature and atmosphere in the car, and roll down the window if it gets too warm and stuffy. Singing to yourself is nice too. Since I can't carry a tune, about the only time I'm free to sing without causing pain to others is when I'm driving. Somehow, it's much more fun than in the shower. On some trips I've gone through every nursery rhyme and children's song I could remember, and then attempted a few hymns and "The Star-Spangled Banner."

I have a workaholic friend who occasionally makes forced night drives to get to the next client on time. Her techniques for keeping awake include eating peanuts. The ones in the shell. She says it keeps her occupied to have to shell them with one hand. The car is always knee-deep in peanut shells, but never mind. She also drives with the radio going full blast and the window wide open. Once at midnight on the New Jersey Turnpike she lit a cigarette with a new, very expensive gold lighter and then absent-mindedly tossed the lighter out the window.

Most women I have talked to dislike two things about freeway driving: big trucks and big cities. Those trucks can be frightening when they overtake you at night in the rain and throw up great waves of muddy water over your windshield. The thing to remember about trucks is that the drivers hate to have to slow down. It may take as many as twelve gear changes and as long as an eighth of a mile to bring one of those giants to a stop. And then they have to go through all the gears again to get back up to speed. Keep your eye out for the trucks and get out of the way early if one wants to pass you. And as it does start to pass, *slow down*. It'll get by you that much sooner, and in bad weather will throw less water or slush up onto your car.

I have found that truck drivers are almost universally courteous. There probably are exceptions, but I haven't met any. Just about the only thing about "civilian" drivers that makes them angry is when a car is tailgating them; they can't see the car but know it's there, and know if they have to stop suddenly the car may smash into the rear of the truck, probably with fatal results. Fatal for the driver of the car, that is. They dislike it too when a car gets in front of the truck and then slows down. It's dangerous for everyone. If the truck is laboring up a long incline at 40 mph (at 40 and under they're supposed to put on their flashers and usually do), the driver will do everything possible to let you pass safely.

Truck drivers may not be the shining knights of the road, as claimed in some country-and-western songs. On the other hand, they're not grimy brutes with rippling muscles and macho tattoos, either. Some are women. The men, often as not, will be seen at the truck stops freshly showered and shaved and wearing silk shirts.

As for the cities, try to time your trip so that you don't arrive in one, or have to pass through one, at rush hour. Even at off times, though, traffic is heaviest here. Most large cities now have ring roads so you can drive past them without getting involved in downtown jams. But the ring roads are a boon to commuters too, so speeds vary a lot as drivers come onto and leave the freeway.

Near cities and on the ring roads, go with the flow of traffic. Local drivers know when an exit is coming up, where the construction is, where the bad curve is, and they drive accordingly. By staying with the flow you'll take advantage of their knowledge and not be forced to change lanes or slow suddenly when you see the sign.

Unless you're looking for your exit on one of these ring roads, it's best to stay in one of the two left-most lanes. That way you'll avoid cars coming on and those slowing for an exit, and will make the best time. Watch out for left-hand exits, though. that's why the center lane may be better than the left one. But if the speed there is too fast for you and makes you uncomfortable, move right and slow down.

Safety

A large number of the comments and recommendations I've already made have to do with safety. Here are some more recommendations.

If you're driving in an unfamiliar area, especially if you're alone, plan ahead. Have a good map and study it. Every single long-distance driver I know keeps a dog-eared Rand McNally Road Atlas in the car. Trace your route ahead of time, and check your progress on the map at each stop. It's much easier if you have a passenger to navigate for you, provided he or she can read a map.

Another time when it's nice to have company is for toll roads. If you haven't yet learned how to tell the difference between a penny and a dime by touch at night, don't let yourself be distracted from driving by trying to find the change as you approach the toll booth. Wait until you've stopped and take the extra time to count out the coins then.

Don't stop on the freeway unless it truly is an emergency. I can think of only two reasons for pulling over onto the shoulder. One is if your car just won't go— you've got a flat tire or the engine quits. (There is no excuse for running out of gas. It's dumb and dangerous and don't let it happen, ever.) The other is if something is in danger of falling off your car. I had to stop once because the trim over the door came loose and was flapping; I was afraid it would fly off altogether and hit another car.

For anything else—to look at a map, take off your jacket, get out the thermos of coffee, or for any non-emergency stop—wait until you can get off the freeway at an exit, a service area, or a rest stop.

No, I just thought of a third reason. If a police car is behind you with his bubble-gum machine lights going.

All the safety guides tell you never, never to back up for an exit. Yet I see this happening at least once a week. What are the idiots thinking of? I even saw a driver once backing up for a left-hand exit. Backing up in the fast lane. I didn't hang around to see if he survived. It's better to go an extra hundred miles, if you have to, than to try a moronic stunt like that. Everyone misses an exit once in a while. Not everyone who backs up for an exit makes it.

Now we come to a question I have been debating with myself and with others for a long time. What do you do when your car breaks down and there's no service station in sight? The standard procedure, given in safety guides, is to get off the road, tie a white cloth to the driver's door handle, put the flashes on, raise the hood, and wait for help. I am not at all convinced that this is the best procedure for a woman alone. You are signaling to any passing freak, weirdo, or nut that you are alone and helpless. The vast majority of those who pass, or stop to help you, will be sane, sober law-abiding, courteous citizens. It only takes one who isn't. Or worse, a carload of them.

Having a CB gives you an option. You can get on the emergency channel (9) and try for help. Or try on the truckers' channel (19), where there may be more listeners. You're still broadcasting that you're stuck, but more people know it and know that others know it, and you're likely to find a police car listening in too.

Another alternative is to leave the car with the flashers on and walk. I would do this only if I knew an exit or a telephone was near, and only in daylight.

Or, you could just sit there with the signals going, but with the doors locked, and not get out of the car unless a police patrol stopped. Sooner or later, a police patrol will see you. If anyone else stops, roll down the window just enough to ask them to go to a telephone to call the police or a service station. This is the option I would choose in most situations.

Never hitchhike.

Never pick up a hitchhiker.

Always lock all doors when you leave the car, even for a few minutes. Keep the doors locked when you're in the car too, especially in slow traffic in cities.

It's sad that those rules are necessary and must be so rigid, but that's the way it is.

Finally, here are three books I recommend; you will no doubt find some others that are equally helpful at the bookstore or library.

What Every Woman Should Know About Her Car, by Dorothy Jackson. Radnor, Pa.: Clifton, 1974. How the engine works, maintenance, and mechanics.

Belts On, Buttons Down: What Every Woman Should Know About Car Safety, by Edward N. Fales, Jr., and members of the staff of Boston Children's Medical Center. New York: Delacorte, 1971. Lost of good advice about driving with children in the car, but recommended even if you don't have children.

Basic Car Care, by A. M. Pettis. New York: Monarch, 1977.

4

Getting There— by Air

I find air travel nothing but tedious. Every airport in the world looks like every other airport in the world. It's very discouraging when you find yourself looking at your ticket as you get off the plane in an effort to remember what city you're in. Airplanes are uncomfortable and boring. But since flying is usually the fastest way to get there, most business travelers fly of necessity.

Flying means, first of all, making the arrangements. United Airlines' statistics, quoted in the introduction, show that more women than men use a travel agent, and that women plan their trips much further in advance. I wish this was because women are better organized, but I suspect that the real reason is that travel is more of a special event for women. For example, United's figures show that 39 percent of female travelers are attending a convention, as opposed to 12 percent of men. Since there are still many more men than women at conventions, this probably means that the convention is the only out-of-town trip the woman will make. Conventions are announced well in advance.

I don't know what the travel agent figures mean. Maybe the woman traveler is sparing her secretary, or maybe she doesn't have a secretary so she uses the travel agent instead. The advantage of a travel agent is that you can make a whole series of reservations—car rentals and hotels as well as flights—in one phone call. But *don't* rely on the agent for choosing the hotel or the flight.

Don't rely on the airlines either. Choose your flight yourself and then call. This is especially important if your trip requires connecting flights. The airline will want to put you on their own flights, whereas if you change airlines midway you might get there hours sooner.

I recently had to get from West-of-No-Where, South Carolina, to Detroit. The travel agency sent over a ticket that showed three connecting flights and a total traveling time of seven and a half hours, of which more than five hours would be spent sitting around in airports waiting. I changed the reservations myself and did the whole trip in three hours.

To do this you need an important resource. It's the *Official Airline Guide*. Your company may subscribe to the large version, which is the size of a telephone book. Whether or not it does, you should have a personal subscription to the pocket version. Write to Reuben H. Donnelley Corp., 2000 Clearwater Drive, Oak Brook, IL 60521. You get a new issue every month. Carry it with you whenever you fly, in your handbag, pocket, or briefcase.

Study the OAG to learn what the codes mean and what kind of information it gives you. For example, it tells you the type of aircraft. Jumbos—wide-body planes—are much more comfortable. These are L1011's and Boeing 747's, usually. So if you have a choice of two flights leaving within a few minutes of each other, you'd pick the wide-body plane over the DC-9 or 727.

The OAG gives connecting flights but not all possible connections. This is important to know. The seven-and-a-half-hour trip booked for me by the travel agent was the one shown in the OAG. I found the alternative by looking up each leg of the trip by city in the OAG. The reason my version wasn't given was that the connections allowed only a short time—in one case, ten minutes—between flights. That's impossible if you have checked luggage or if one flight is late. I was lucky on that trip; in fact, one departing flight was at the gate right beside my arriving flight.

The OAG is invaluable too if your meeting has run late and you've missed the flight you had a reservation on, or if your flight is delayed and you need an alternative, or if you miss a connection for any reason. You just whip it out and start looking for the next available flight.

Fares

It can be useful for you to know something about fare structures and pricing policies, even when you're a business traveler and cost isn't a primary consideration. There are so many different "special plans" and they change so rapidly that I'm not even going to try to summarize them here. But knowing what kinds of bargains you can get is useful if you're planning to add a vacation on to a business trip, for example. Or you might take advantage of special deals for your own convenience. For instance, several airlines let you sit in first-class with a full-fare coach ticket on a night flight. Ask a travel agent or the airline about special fares.

Stand-By and Wait-List Options

If you can't get a reservation on the flight you want, use the wait-list. Each airline has a slightly different procedure for this, but generally speaking you can get on a wait-list by phone ahead of time, and on a stand-by list when you actually arrive at the airport. As cancellations are received the available seats are given out on a first-come, first-served basis, so the earlier you get your name in the better. At the airport you won't know until the last minute whether you'll get on the flight, since it will depend on the number of no-shows.

If you can't get any reservation at all, the stand-by method is your only chance for getting away, with the alternative being to spend an extra night where you are. In that case, get your name on the wait-list for every single possible flight out to your destination, including flights that go to cities where you might get a connection for your final destination. The OAG is invaluable for plotting this.

The busiest flying times are around holidays and on Friday nights and Monday mornings. I once wanted to get from Indianapolis to Boston on the Wednesday night before Thanksgiving. Everything was fully booked. I got on a flight to Baltimore as a stand-by passenger on a plane that was continuing to Boston. I was told that they would have to put me off the plane in Baltimore because the flight was already overbooked and passengers holding confirmed reservations would have priority. I would have priority over all stand-by passengers waiting in Baltimore, however. When the plane landed I just sat tight, trying to be invisible, as the new passengers got on. Sure enough, no one said a word to me and I got to Boston for the holiday on time.

In fact, you are quite likely to get a seat at holiday rush periods. Many travelers then are non-business persons, such as students, who are apt to change their plans at the last minute because they were offered a ride or found some other activity that looked more interesting.

Using the stand-by procedure can aid you when you are making a connection and your first flight sets down *early*. Yes, it does happen sometimes, especially on longer flights and when the pilot is able to take advantage of prevailing winds. You might then get a flight out earlier than the one you were booked on. Having only carry-on luggage is essential for this trick. Several times I have cut an hour and a half off the travel time between the East Coast to Seattle by getting an earlier connection out of O'Hare in Chicago.

Knowing the system can make it work for you. There is one no-no, though: don't double-book. A few professional travelers do it, but it's not to anyone's advantage. It starts the spiral that makes the airlines think they have to overbook because they'll have no-shows, and that leads to bumping, which causes more passengers to double-book....

Delays and Bumping

Two of the most infuriating things that can happen are having your flight delayed, and getting bumped. If I had to choose, I'd say bumping was worse because you don't know it's happened until the last minute. You rush up to the gate with your ticket—a confirmed reservation—in your hand and are told, "Sorry, we don't have any seats." They overbooked the flight and you're stuck. This is one reason for getting to the airport and getting checked in early, but if you're arriving on a connecting flight there's nothing you can do to prevent it.

The regulations change from time to time, so keep yourself informed about what the airline is obliged to do in cases like this. Right now, if you're bumped you get back the price of your ticket *and* are given priority on the next possible flight out on any airline. If the next flight is a certain number of hours away, they have to give you a cash compensation too. There is one new procedure that helps: the airline will ask for volunteers to be bumped.

Three of us got out of Pittsburgh this way recently, when a family volunteered to be bumped instead. They were quite pleased about it, in fact, because they were very tired and not in a hurry to get home. They got a free dinner and hotel and a free flight the next day and I and my companions got home that night.

Also know what your rights are if the flight is delayed in leaving. Generally, you have a lot more owed to you if you've already checked in, which is another reason for getting there early. It's ominous when they suddenly stop checking in passengers who are waiting in line. It means there's going to be a delay and they don't know for how long. Be skeptical about announcements that it will be only ten minutes. I once sat at JFK for four hours' worth of ten-minute delays. Every twenty minutes they'd announce another ten-minutes' delay. The aircraft needed a repair and there was no other one available. The airline's later flights for the same destination were departing on time and full; from the carrier's point of view this was the best policy, because if it had taken one of those planes for us, it would have had to deal with *two* lots of angry passengers instead of just one.

Many of the other passengers on my flight were tourists who didn't know what the airline was required to do for them if they asked. I got a free telegram to my hotel to hold my room, and a free phone call to the person meeting me to save her a needless trip to the airport. The tourists were lined up at the pay phones. If the delay had been any longer, the airline would have had to pay my hotel bill for the night—at *two* hotels, the one where I was and the one where I was supposed to be.

Arriving at the wrong airport is maddening too. I was once again on a trip to Boston when the flight was diverted to Providence because of bad weather. That was one time when I had checked luggage and wished heartily that I hadn't; the airline wouldn't unload the luggage for the whole three hours we sat in Providence. I could have rented a car and gotten to Boston in an hour by road if I'd been willing to leave all my things behind.

In all of these situations, having the OAG in your handbag or briefcase can be a real advantage. It may not always save the day, but it gives you a fighting chance.

Where to Sit

Experienced travelers always ask for an aisle seat and let the tourists have the window. The thrill of looking at clouds from above wears off very rapidly, and if by chance there really is a spectacular view on landing or takeoff, you can still get a good look at it from the aisle seat. An aisle seat is much more comfortable because you can stretch out your legs a little and have more room on one side for your arm. Just be careful that you're not blocking the aisle with your feet or with your carry-on bag. A further advantage is that you can get up to go to the toilet, get a magazine, or whatever without disturbing the other passengers. This helps on a crowded flight because you can go to the toilet right after you finish eating, when there's no line for it. In a window seat, you're trapped by the trays until the flight attendant comes back to take them away, which is exactly the moment when ninety-five other passengers decide to use the toilet too.

Some people take it even further and ask for a left-side aisle seat if they're right-handed, and vice versa, so they will have elbow room for their writing arm.

If you can't get an aisle seat, a window seat is second choice, because at least there's no one else on one side of you. A center seat is the least desirable. (If you're stuck with one because you were late checking in, consider murdering another passenger, but make sure you don't pick someone who also has a center seat.) I take a window seat as first choice only when I'm ill or very tired and want to sleep. You can rest your head against the cabin wall, and with enough pillows and blankets you can get comfortable enough to be able to doze off. Unless I'm truly exhausted or running a fever, though, I can't sleep on a plane. I envy those who can.

Some experienced passengers will try to hog an aisle seat when they've actually been assigned the center one. They're hoping that if you're the one with the aisle, you'll be too inexperienced or too timid to argue and you'll take the center. Don't. You've got your boarding pass with the seat number right on it, and you can call the flight attendant, if necessary, to arbitrate.

Now we come to the back-versus-front debate. Since the introduction of separate smoking sections the debate has dwindled somewhat, because the issue is decided for smokers and for nonsmokers who don't want to sit in the smoking section. The only ones who have a full choice are nonsmokers who don't mind being with smokers. Smoking seats usually are at the back of the plane, generally considered the least desirable half to sit in, which seems fair enough to me. The most comfortable seats, in terms of the smoothness of the flight, are forward and over the wings. Some travelers believe that the back row and the front row are the safest in the case of a crash, but I've never seen any statistics to prove it. I'd just as soon be near an emergency exit.

A passenger traveling with a baby often gets the front seat or the one just behind the bulkhead because that's where they can hang a baby carrier. This is very nice for the adult with the infant. What business travelers hate most on planes are babies and little kids. Even if devoted parents themselves, they'll moan and snarl if there are children on board. I feel sorry for babies especially, because you can't tell them to yawn or blow their nose to make their ears stop hurting. But I hate it just as much as the other passengers when an infant screams steadily for an hour and a half. So if you see babies getting on the plane, try for a rear seat where you have a chance of being as far away from them as possible. Unless it's your baby, of course. Well, even then—you could pretend you weren't together.

If you're going to have to run when you land, get a front seat so you can be first off the plane. If the flight you're on is late and it's going to be tight making your connection, move to a forward seat before landing. If all seats are occupied, tell the flight attendant and try to arrange a swap with a passenger who has checked luggage and isn't in a hurry.

A final word on seating when there's more than one of you. With two, if you want to talk, get adjacent aisle seats. Three is very difficult. If you must try to hold a discussion, one will have to be a martyr and take the center. It's impossible to hold a four-way conversation on a plane, so you might as well sit in different rows. (The exception would be on those few aircraft that have backward-facing seats, but you can't count on that.)

Last-Minute Panics

In spite of my comments about the advantages of getting to the airport early, I rarely do it myself because I hate sitting and waiting. My ultimate goal, which I rarely achieve, is to time it so that I can walk to my gate at a brisk pace, but not running, be the last passenger checked in and aboard, and have the doors close for takeoff as I sit down. I worked with a man who took this philosophy one step further, reasoning that if he cut it fine enough, one time in ten he'd miss the plane, but it was worth it for not having to sit around and wait the other nine times. It was maddening to travel with him because I never knew whether he was going to arrive at a dead run and fall into his seat panting, or whether this was the tenth time and he wouldn't make it.

I have to say it just once more; you save time by not having any luggage to check. If you have your ticket too, never bother to wait in line at the outside counter to check in, no matter what the airline would like. Find your gate on the TV monitor or the board and go straight there to check in and get your seat, if there's seat selection.

If you have to check your luggage or pick up your

ticket and you're late arriving, don't stand in a long line. You may miss the plane. My technique is to jump the queue and get the attention of any clerk behind the counter who isn't talking to a passenger. I tell them I'm in danger of missing the plane, or that I just want to get my ticket which is waiting for me, and I usually get fast service. I don't know how ethical that is, but no one's ever hit me over the head with an umbrella. On those days when by mistake I'm there in plenty of time, I'm patient in the line and let passengers with earlier flights push ahead.

If you're traveling with a companion and rushing to reach the gate, use the technique called "one carries, one runs." One of you takes all the carry-on stuff, and the other one, unencumbered, does the O. J. Simpson routine to get to the gate. All that's necessary is for one of you to get there before they close the door of the plane. You can pretend to faint in the doorway if you have to, while the carrier catches up. This is worth a try even if the clock says you've already missed it. I haven't done a study with a stopwatch, but I'd be willing to bet that more than half of all flights don't close the doors at the scheduled time.

Safety

We had just landed and our pilot was making an announcement. "Ladies and gentlemen," he said, "the safest part of your journey is now over. If you're driving the rest of the way, please be careful." He was absolutely right, of course. Any way you measure it, air travel is the safest mode of commercial transportation there is. Bad crashes make the headlines only because so many people die at once.

If you're terrified in a plane, you have four choices. Keep flying and keep on being terrified. Stop flying, and find another job that doesn't require it. Get psychological help—the fear is not really rational because statistically you have more reason to be petrified in a car or even just crossing the street. Or try to work it out for yourself. I have one friend who has done this. For years, every plane journey was an agony for him. He says, "I finally decided I had to choose between not flying at all, which would have limited my job and personal life very much, or I had to overcome it. I couldn't stand the strain any longer. I decided to stop being afraid, and worked at it, telling myself all the rational things. It took awhile, but gradually my fears lessened and now it doesn't bother me at all." In most crashes, either everybody survives or no one does, so my attitude is that it's not worth worrying about.

I think that one of the reasons some people are irrationally afraid in a plane is because they feel helpless, with no control. There is, however, one very practical measure you can take to improve your safety. That is to wear your seat belt all the time you're sitting down. It's true when the airlines say that most experienced travelers do this, even when the seat belt sign is off.

I'll explain further about seat belts by telling an anecdote. I was traveling with a man I worked with. There was some turbulence, but he'd undone his seat belt. The flight attendant came along and suggested he put it on. He said, "Give me one good reason why I should."

"All right," she replied, "I will. Last year I was on a flight with my best friend, when we had turbulence just like this. She should have had her belt on but didn't. The plane hit an air pocket and dropped suddenly. She hit the cabin roof and it broke her neck."

"That's a very good reason," he said, and he fastened his belt.

Although it's rare, it is possible to encounter CAT—clear-air turbulence—without any warning. Use your belt.

Some people believe that being able to swim will improve your chances in case of an emergency landing in water. Swimming is a useful skill in any case.

The only other active measure you can take that I know of is to pay attention to the instructions and demonstration given at the start of the flight about the oxygen masks and the emergency doors. It's hard to avoid doing this until you're thoroughly sick of it anyway.

I'm sometimes asked about the advisability of taking out those one-trip insurance policies that are sold at most airports. My opinion is that since they're so cheap, if it makes you feel better it can't hurt. Selling that kind of insurance is like a license to print money, however, because the statistics are very much in favor of the insurance company never having to pay out. I know a few people who use the policies like greeting cards—pop a few in the mail to friends every trip to say they're thinking of them.

It would be more practical to check your own life insurance policies and the insurance you get through your employer. Many companies have special insurance that covers you just on company travel, in addition to the policy you may have as a job-related benefit. Check on all of these to find out whether they cover you on charter flights, nonscheduled flights, air taxis and commuter lines, and in private or company-owned planes. If there are loopholes, you might consider a special travel policy to fill the gap. Again, this type of insurance is very cheap, with the possible exception of coverage on privately owned planes.

Some organizations have a special rule that limits how many of their senior executives may travel on one aircraft at a time. Several companies have suffered severe business setbacks when all their key executives, or all their top salesmen, were killed in one crash. I know several married couples who use the same principle. Either the whole family travels together, or the husband and wife take different flights. This improves the odds that their children will not lose both parents at the same time. It makes sense to me.

Comfort

The best things you can do to make the flight as comfortable as possible for yourself are to choose a wide-body plane and choose an aisle seat. If you can sleep on a plane, there are always blankets and pillows the flight attendant will bring. If it's a long flight, get your share early.

Uncrowded flights are much better too, but you don't always have a choice. I have sometimes taken the west-east "red-eye special" when many seats were unoccupied. This is terrific, because you can push up the armrests and have three or more seats all to yourself. I can sleep that way, stretched out on three seats. I use the ends of two different seat belts to hold me in case of turbulence, and lots of pillows and blankets.

It's considered OK to take off your shoes on a flight. Wear comfortable ones, and if you take them off be sure your feet aren't swelling. This happens with some people and they have trouble getting their shoes back on.

On a long flight, think about your eyes too. The humidity on planes is very low, often only 2 or 3 percent. This affects your eyes first, making them feel dry and fatigued. Try eye drops. I found it uncomfortable to wear hard contact lenses for more than an hour while flying, but my new soft lenses are better.

There's another problem that air travelers don't talk about very much, and I don't know any solution for it. This is gas and flatulence caused, I guess, by the cabin pressure. (I've never asked, but I suspect this is one of the reasons for the stale but perfumed atmosphere on planes.)

Everyone has their own solution to the problem of ears popping from the altitude and pressure. These include blowing the nose with the mouth closed, chewing gum, sucking on a piece of candy, snuffing on a menthol inhaler, and simulated yawning. I usually go through the whole repertoire. I find it actually painful only when I have a head cold. The menthol inhaler helps best then.

Before landing, especially on long flights, it can freshen you up enormously to take your whole toilet kit into the rest room and do a complete job on your face. Plan this so you don't leave it until the last minute with other passengers waiting for a turn and the pilot telling you over the address system to return to your seat for landing. Be sure to include lots of moisturizer, because of the low humidity. I know some people who change clothes, too, but I feel that only movie stars and politicians can get away with that without appearing a little silly.

Within the continental United States, the longest possible flight takes three hours, not long enough to cause serious jet lag in most people. I'll discuss jet lag and what to do about it in the chapter on overseas travel.

A few words about courtesy to other passengers. I assume you'll observe the basic rules of politeness, but there are things that are annoying to others that you might not know about. One of these is clutching the backs of seats as you walk down the aisle. It may be necessary to keep from losing your balance, but do try to use the overhead rack or the backs of empty seats if you can. I especially hate it when someone accidentally pulls my hair. Similarly, when you stand up put your hand on the back of *your own* seat for support, rather than grabbing the back of the seat in front.

I try not to tip my "reclining" seat back because it

reduces the room of the person behind. On short flights, it adds very little to your comfort anyway. If you do have the seat back, bring it up when food or beverages are served so the person behind you doesn't have to eat with his dinner jutting into his chest.

And finally, if you are being persistently annoyed, ask the person to stop, and if that doesn't work, call the flight attendant. I am thinking of such things as having the back of your seat repeatedly kicked by a teenager wearing ski boots, being used as a pillow by the drunk beside you, or having someone light up a big black cigar in the nonsmoking section when you're allergic to the stuff.

Special Situations

I once had to fly home from Europe on an hour's notice at the peak of the vacation season because my mother was dying. The airline, BOAC, was absolutely marvelous in doing everything they could to help, including giving me a seat in the first-class section, where there is more privacy, though I had a coach ticket. If you have a personal or business emergency, tell the airline and the flight attendants about it. Even if you think there's nothing they can do, they may know of procedures that could help get you there sooner or otherwise make things easier. But they can't do anything if you don't tell them.

I'm not saying much about traveling with babies and children in this book because I'm assuming most women won't have them along on business trips. In case you do, though, you should know that the airlines will do all kinds of extra things for you. They (unlike the passengers) love kids, because they're the business travelers of the future. The kids' meals, hot dogs and hamburgers, always look a lot more appetizing than what is served to the rest of us. And the coloring books!—but I've always been too timid to ask for one for myself, no matter how bored I was. I've even seen the flight attendant putting up a curtain around a seat so a nursing mother could have privacy. The airlines are very good with unaccompanied children too.

If you're pregnant, you should of course check with your doctor about flying. Most airlines will take you up to the seventh month. They get very nervous about it though; other than a mechanical problem with the aircraft, a passenger with a medical emergency is one of the things they dread most. If you're over six months or look like you might be, go armed with a note from your doctor. Try to keep with the crowd when you check in and stand as close as you can to the counter so the agent doesn't get a good look. They're usually so harassed that they never look at you anyway. The only other advice I can think of is to be as brazen as possible.

A final word. Even if you don't hate flying as much as I do, you probably wouldn't swap your job for that of a flight attendant. It is not as glamorous as recruitment ads of earlier years made out. If the journey has been trouble-free and the service efficient, say thank you or something else nice as you get off the plane. More than once, I've seen a tired and unhappy looking face light up because a passenger said something nice.

5

Lodging

The subject of lodging is not as extensive as some others I have been dealing with in this book. Especially on brief trips, when you're on business your hotel room is just a place to sleep at night, not a "home." It can become more important if you're at one site for a long time, or if you travel almost all the time. I'll talk about those circumstances in the chapter on corporate gypsies.

Very often your choice of hotel will be predetermined: you're visiting one of your company's locations and visitors are always booked into a certain place; or you're at a convention and will naturally stay where it's being held. Many large companies have special arrangements with the larger motel chains for business rates on rooms, so you stay at one of those.

If you're not sure, or if you have a choice, the best bet is to call and ask someone at the location you'll be visiting for advice. Even though the locals don't stay in the motels themselves, they'll know about food and have feedback from other visitors. While you're on the phone, get travel directions too, if you'll be arriving at the hotel by car.

When you have no other way to choose, you will probably do best with one of the large chains. As one of the ads says, there aren't any surprises. Just like airports, all Holiday Inns look alike. They're all fairly modern and have a basic standard of comfort.

However, if you have a choice or the chance to get some local information, ask about individually owned or family-owned hotels or inns; they are often much better places to stay. The service is more individual, as is the decor. In addition, I usually feel more secure in a place like that. The staff knows who I am. You can be at one of the lookalike chain motels for three weeks, and none of the staff knows you by sight.

Any place in or near a big city requires a reservation. You can't take a chance on being able to get a room by walking in; there might be a convention in town or some other special event. Specify what time you'll be arriving; if in doubt, ask for a guaranteed late arrival. That means they'll hold your room no matter what. If you don't show up you'll still have to pay for it, so if something goes wrong at the last minute be sure to call.

On the road, you can take your chances if you want. That's what I do, because I don't like to have to commit myself to getting to a certain point by a certain time. If the weather's bad I may want to stop sooner, or if I feel like it I may want to push on for an extra hundred miles that night. I've never had to sleep in the car, but there have been a few times when there wasn't much choice by the time I started looking. I know some women who make firm reservations right across the country in advance, in order not to get stuck without a place to sleep.

When you're on the road like that, you again have a choice of the standard chains or of truckers' motels. You'll find these at or near the big truck-stop service areas. They are sometimes part of a chain, sometimes privately owned, almost always cheaper. I've always found them to be comfortable and interesting places to stay and have never had any problems. Unlike the Holiday Inns, individual places stand out in my mind. There was one in Montana, for example, that had an extensive paperback book collection in the lobby; you borrowed what you wanted and left the ones you'd read behind. It was a charming idea. In another place, in Oregon, there were nondenominational church services on Sunday morning right in the motel. Many have free coffee and "on your honor" snack bars.

It may sometimes happen that you arrive with a confirmed reservation and they tell you they haven't got a room for you. If you're reserving well in advance, always ask for a confirming letter and take it with you. Or, if you've made the reservation through a travel agency, you'll have the confirmation from them. *In extremis* remember that all large hotels *always* have a few extra rooms, even when they say they're full. One time in Chicago, I got so angry when they denied any knowledge of my reservation that I started unpacking my bag in the lobby in preparation for sleeping on the couch there. They suddenly "found" my reservation. Once in Cincinnati I didn't have a reservation but bluffed my way in because other people from my company were staying there. I said that if they had rooms for everyone else, how could they have overlooked me? It turned out that they did have a room after all.

Safety

There are certain precautions you should take in a hotel or motel. The first is to keep your room number to yourself. I don't like it at all when the clerk hands me my key and loudly announces the room number to the crowd around the desk. One woman I work with gets so upset by this that she'll walk away, and then go back when the crowd has cleared and ask for a different room. Similarly, don't advertise your room number in the bar or restaurant if you're signing the check.

I've already said it several times, and will again. Always double-lock your hotel room door and put the chain on. If you're on the ground floor or have a balcony, check the windows and the sliding door, if there is one. If you can't lock it, call the front desk to have them send a maintenance person to show you how it works or to fix it if it's broken.

If I'm feeling the least bit doubtful about the door lock, or if I just happen to be a little paranoid that week, I get all the keys to my room. This is easy. It's a nuisance to hand in your room key whenever you leave, and absolutely unnecessary, no matter what the hotel people say. Only tourists do it, and after their first experience of having to wait in line ten minutes to get the key back, they don't bother either. So keep the first key you're issued all the time.

Then, the first time I go out, I stop at the front desk and ask for my key. There's always a second one, sometimes more. I've never been questioned—"Don't you already have a key?"—but if I were, I'd say I'd mislaid it or left it in my room. Then I check the box behind the desk to see if any keys are left, and keep repeating this routine until I have them all. This doesn't inconvenience the hotel in the slightest; the housekeeping staff have passkeys. When I check out I hand all the keys back in again without explanation.

I've kept count, and only about 60 percent of the time does the person at the front desk ask my name and check the guest list to see if it really is *my* room I want the key for.

Don't enter your room if there are persons nearby in the corridor about whom you are doubtful. Fiddle around, or walk past and double back. Similarly, when leaving take a quick look up and down the corridor before you step out of the door. And then check that the door has locked behind you.

In most places there will be a notice posted in your

room saying that the establishment is not responsible for valuables, that these may be left with the manager. They mean it. Larger places have individual safe-deposit boxes, just like a bank. Or they'll put your stuff in the office safe. I have used this service several times when I had, for various reasons, large amounts of cash, jewelry, or legal documents that needed protection. I always felt that I got special attention afterward, as a person with something important enough to keep in the safe—probably just ego-tripping on my part. If you're going to do this, put the stuff in an envelope or package and seal it. It's none of their business what it is you're storing. Sign your name on the package, across the seal if possible.

I'm of two minds about whether belongings are safer in your car or in the hotel room. I started keeping everything in my room the week one of our accountants had his car stolen from outside his motel, and then stopped the day I got back from work and found the door of the room open. The chambermaid had neglected to close it after finishing. Now I divide things between the car and the room, on the theory that I'm less likely to lose everything at once.

Services

It's surprising how few people know of the variety of services most larger hotels and motels offer. Taking advantage of them can make life easier. Everyone knows about room service, of course, and the valet; and I've already mentioned locking up your valuables.

The housekeeping department can be useful too. It will often supply you with an iron and an ironing board, which saves on valet charges or gives you a chance for a quick press when you don't want to wait. Housekeeping can also give you extra pillows, blankets, towels, needle and thread, and the like. (A tip is expected.)

Call for maintenance if there's a problem with the heat, air conditioning, windows, doors, lighting, TV, or plumbing. The first two are particularly tricky. Don't feel timid about calling the front desk or the maintenance department if you can't make them work. If you can't, thousands of others have had the same problem too. A tip is *not* appropriate in this case—things should work.

I've found that the personal service in non-chain places is usually excellent. In various places their services have included providing a bedboard for a too-soft bed, storing my extra luggage when I was going to be away just for the weekend, and sending someone out to the drug store for me when I was sick. (I'll have more to say about this in the chapter on health, but do remember that every hotel has a doctor on call for emergencies.)

Alternative Lodging

Staying in a private house with friends or relatives is much nicer than using a hotel or motel, of course. Sometimes, though, you'll want to choose the hotel anyway because you're carrying on business there. But if you do stay in someone's house, check on what your company's expense account policy is. You may be able to pay your friends the equivalent of the hotel cost, or at least buy them a nice present on the company. Everybody wins in this situation. You're more comfortable, the company saves some money, and your friends get something out of it.

I'll discuss other alternatives, renting or subletting a house or apartment, in Chapter 12.

6
Food

Eating right while you are traveling can be difficult. If you're away only a few days a month, it doesn't matter if you're eating too much or eating junk, as long as you're sensible the rest of the time. On longer trips, or if you have a weight or health problem that requires a stricter diet, you can be in trouble if you're not careful.

Restaurants

There are several problems. One is that, when you're eating in restaurants all the time, you are surrounded by temptation. Another is that you may have little to say about the type of restaurants you go to. When you are, in a sense, a "guest" of the people at the site you are visiting, it is ungracious and may be politically unwise to refuse to go to their "best restaurant in town," especially if you are not picking up the check. Once there, it seems impolite to refuse the recommended specialty. For the people you are visiting, it may be an occasion that calls for a fancier lunch than they would normally have. For you, it can mean an extra ten pounds by the time you get home.

Why is it that regional specialties are almost always fattening? It sounds downright unpatriotic to turn down black-bottom pie in Atlanta, gumbo in New Orleans, or beer and cheese in Milwaukee.

Even when you think you're ordering something low-calorie and sensible, there may be traps. Broiled fish is almost always cooked in butter and may have extra butter poured over it; one tablespoon of butter has 100 calories, so 400 to 500 calories may be added in this way. Roast chicken may be served with gravy and stuffing. Vegetables may have had baking soda added to the cooking water, which makes the color very nice but destroys most of the nutritional value. You have no control over the size of portions. Toast arrives already buttered, and there's almost always that terrible basket of rolls plunked down on the table before you even order.

As a general rule of thumb, never say you are on a diet. (The exception may be if you have a severe medical problem and *have* to enlist the cooperation of others to keep from going into a coma or breaking out in hives.) Even though more and more male executives these days are on weight-control programs (or should be), talking about a diet still seems to many men to be "feminine" and therefore undesirable in a business context. Even if *they* spend the entire lunch hour discussing calories and jogging, you can establish a certain superiority just by keeping your mouth shut. Superwoman . . . with a weight problem? Never.

If you are one of those people who can skip breakfast and make it through to lunchtime without getting dizzy, do so. Unless you order dry toast, *one* boiled egg, and hold the home fries (or, in the South, the grits), it is impossible to get a restaurant breakfast that doesn't have 600 or 700 calories. Juice and coffee is just fine. If you must eat something, have one of those little boxes of cereal. Ordinarily, I would consider it more nutritious to eat the box and throw away the cereal, but in restaurants this is often the only way to get something with a known, controlled calorie content. Special K has more protein than most cereals; but stay away from the sugared types.

Salad bars are becoming extremely popular in all parts of the country. If the restaurant you are taken to has one, this is the obvious choice for lunch. Go easy on the starchy side dishes like potato salad. Unfortunately, as yet, very few places offer a low-calorie dressing. A noncreamy type, or plain oil and vinegar, will probably be the best choice. Go easy on it, and if you are counting calories estimate 50 per tablespoonful, or 250 per average ladle. Most places have salads on the menu; just be careful of the hidden "extras" like mayonnaise.

The average restaurant dinner works out to 1200–

1500 calories (without drinks—alcohol is discussed later), assuming you eat everything (bread and butter, potatoes). Meat servings are often too large. A plain steak is *not* diet food. An 8-ounce sirloin, which is smallish in some restaurants, will be 600 calories with all the fat trimmed off, closer to 1,000 with the fat.

If, like me, you were brought up by parents who remember the Depression, it may be extremely difficult for you to stop eating when you are no longer hungry, leaving food on the plate. Just remind yourself that you are not going to keep anyone from starving by eating everything, and that you are not a human garbage can. It helps if you feel it is socially OK to ask for a doggy bag. A hunk of cold steak or liver is an excellent breakfast. If the weather is hot, keep it near the air conditioner in your hotel room overnight and it will be perfectly fine to eat in the morning. (Don't keep it any longer than that without refrigeration, of course.)

Here is a battle plan for eating dinner in a restaurant every evening without turning into a hippopotamus. These suggestions go for lunchtime too, if you don't have a salad:

- Pretend the breadbasket is poison. Actually, the butter is worse than the bread. Eat a breadstick or wafer if there are any.
- If a dinner salad comes with the meal, ask for the dressing on the side. Otherwise, it may be drenched.
- No appetizer. A glass of juice may double for your pre-dinner drink and appetizer (discussed later).

- Roast fowl, broiled meat, and boiled seafood (as in shrimp cocktail) are best. Broiled fish is technically good, but you have no control over the amount of butter on it. In terms of a calorie/nutrition balance, pan-fried liver is number one. It is low enough in calories (half that of steak, ounce for ounce) to make the butter used in cooking it tolerable.
- No potato. In deference to the potato growers, it must be said that a potato by itself is not high in calories. At home, you can make a palatable topping for baked potato with yogurt and herbs. In a restaurant, it is impossible to get one that hasn't had the calories doubled or tripled by being cooked in fat, or by butter being added later. If you can eat a baked potato plain, fine, but I've never met anyone who could.
- Judiciously chosen vegetables.
- No dessert.

The posher the restaurant, the easier it is, socially, to ask for exceptions like salad dressing on the side or broiled instead of fried fish, even if it isn't on the menu.

I once patronized an exclusive French restaurant in London. It was an "in" place, and reportedly some member of the royal family could be seen there any weekend. (I never saw the Queen, however.) We took business clients there because it impressed them, and because it was quiet on weekday evenings. One night when business was slow the proprietor sat down for an after-dinner drink with us.

As any tourist would have done given the opportunity, I asked him what the royals ate. He said that they almost never ordered from the menu or even looked at it, much to the disgust of the chef, who labored so hard over his specialties. They usually would have something very plain, like an omelet or broiled sole. Any top-class restaurant will make you any simple dish you ask for, provided they have the ingredients on hand, and you can be sure it will be good.

Acting on this principle, I once asked for a plain tomato salad in a restaurant in New York. It was prepared as a labor of love, each slice perfect, garnished with a sprinkle of chopped parsley and a paper-thin slice of onion, and served with style. It was the best-tasting tomato I ever ate.

Fruit and Vegetables

Another nutrition problem on the road is getting enough *fresh* food, especially raw fruits and vegetables (other than salad). In many restaurants, "fresh" on the menu means "fresh frozen," and this is apparently quite legal in most places. It is no good asking the waiter or waitress if the item is really fresh; these people probably don't know, and will say what they think you want to hear anyway. You know very well that the "fresh" scallops on a menu in Ohio are going to be frozen; either that, or they've been flown in and the price will be astronomical. Even in areas with fresh, seasonal local produce, most things will be frozen. Very few restaurants will go to the trouble of cutting and weighing meat, or cleaning and trimming vegetables, if they can buy prepackaged portion-controlled frozen food. It saves them time, and they don't have to throw anything away if the item was a slow mover that day. The exceptions are watery foods like lettuce and strawberries, which can't be frozen without changing their character drastically.

I sometimes get so hungry for raw vegetables that a well-cared-for lawn looks appetizing to me. I worked with one woman who would stop at the supermarket and buy fresh broccoli or cauliflower, wash it in the sink in her hotel room, and stand there eating it out of her hand, plain. For breakfast. That seemed a little drastic to me, but I understood how she felt. I usually rely on the lunchtime salad bar and try to get as much variety as possible. I have been known to compose a salad mostly of carrot curls and cucumber slices instead of lettuce.

Fruit, too. The "fresh" fruit salad on menus usually consists partly, or entirely, of frozen or canned fruit, doused in sugar or sugary syrup. You can stave off scurvy with a glass of orange juice, grapefruit juice, or tomato juice every day, but that gets boring and doesn't provide any fiber. The only solution is to bring it with you or buy it locally, wherever you are. Apples travel well and keep well; for a week's trip, put a couple in your suitcase. Eating the local fruit in season can be a real treat. I once spent the month of August working in Washington (the state), near the Canadian border. On the way back to the hotel from work, I passed a farm stand. I feasted every night on the local strawberries and raspberries, fresh picked and still warm from the sun.

Many fruits are available year-round anywhere in the country. I know one man who stops at the supermarket on Monday and buys a bag of grapefruit, wherever he is. He peels one and eats it, just like an orange, for breakfast every morning. He says they will keep for a week in a hotel room. Never mind what the chambermaid will think, seeing a pile of grapefruit on your dresser; chambermaids have seen much stranger sights than that, believe me.

Do It Yourself

Here is my basic eating kit for traveling:

- Combination corkscrew and can opener.
- Jar of instant coffee. I *have* to have coffee first thing in the morning. I used to carry a mug too, until I discovered that you really can boil water (see next item) in those disposable plastic hotel glasses. They sometimes get a little lopsided from the heat, but that's all right.
- Immersion heater for boiling water.
- Spoon.
- Penknife. The blade is good for peeling fruit. Mine is a Swiss Army knife that also has a tiny pair of scissors. You wouldn't believe how often that knife has come in handy. I once loaned out the scissors three different times to three different men at one

hotel-room cocktail party. One wanted to trim a broken nail, another had a loose thread, and the third never did say what he wanted it for, but claimed it was urgent.

The knife is always in my handbag; the other items I pack in my cosmetics kit. You can add things to this list. For example, if you like cream or sugar in your coffee, take packets of sugar or low-calorie sweetener and a small jar of nondairy powdered creamer.

If you want to eat in your hotel room in the evening on occasion, but don't want a full meal from room service, here are some items to take with you or buy at the local supermarket:

- Fresh fruit.
- Yogurt or cottage cheese. Remember the spoon. Obviously, you buy this on site and eat it right away.
- Can of sardines, tuna, or salmon.
- Instant soup, the kind where you boil the water first and then empty the packet into it. Having this available can be very comforting if you're sick and stuck in a hotel room.
- If the supermarket has a deli section, you can get small portions of things like chicken or shrimp salad, chopped liver, and cole slaw. Again, don't leave these hanging around unrefrigerated; anything made with mayonnaise should be eaten promptly.

With just the equipment I have described, and a grocery store or supermarket within driving distance, it is possible to eat nutritionally sound meals in a hotel room forever, without a kitchen. You would probably die of boredom in a week or two, however.

On Planes

Eating on airplanes: don't. Some people won't drink anything alcoholic either, because alcohol seems to metabolize more quickly on a plane. Stick to coffee, which is usually not too bad, and soft drinks. On most flights you will be able to get low-calorie soda or skim milk.

On long flights, especially transatlantic ones, you may *have* to eat or else walk off the plane with an advanced case of low blood sugar, not the best condition in which to deal with immigration and customs officials. You could take your own brown-bag lunch with you, which I have done, but it doesn't seem very chic. On the other hand, big names in the food world such as Julia Child and Craig Claiborne are said to be so appalled by airline food that they recommend packing your own gourmet picnic basket to take on board. So if they can do it, maybe I should change my attitude on this point.

The alternative is to order a special meal in advance. All airlines offer this service at no charge. I recently had an interesting conversation about this with an airline chef. My theory was that the best food to order would be Kosher. He disagreed, and recommended asking for a diabetic's meal. He said that on his airline, and on most others that he knew about, a diabetic's meal is prepared individually and is all fresh food. And, of course, it will be low in carbohydrates. I haven't yet had a chance to test this, but it is certain that nothing could be worse than the standard fare.

The only problem in ordering a special meal is the possibility that they will forget to put your meal on the plane. You'd be stuck; it wouldn't quite do to wave your hand airily and say, "Oh, just bring me any old thing." I once sat beside a young Jewish couple, honeymooners, on a flight to London. The airline had forgotten their Kosher meals, and they would eat absolutely nothing else. I felt so sorry for them; they huddled together holding hands and looking miserable for the whole flight. But I suppose young love can conquer anything, even starvation.

Freeway Eating

When you are traveling by road on a recreational or vacation trip, just about the nicest way to get your meals is to have breakfast in the town where you stopped for the night, then find a grocery store or deli and put together a picnic lunch. You find a scenic spot for your lunch, and the kids and dogs can have a nice romp while you enjoy the view. For dinner, you pore over your guidebooks and choose a picturesque inn or famous local restaurant.

That is all very nice if you have the time, the inclination, and the kids and dogs. On a business trip you usually just want to get there and then get back. For you, "Scenic View" is only a sign that flashes past on the freeway—except in California, where it's "Vista Point." (It took me about a hundred miles to figure out that "Vista Point" wasn't the name of the town. Similarly, many tourists in Germany come back thinking that Ausgang [Exit] is Europe's largest city.) On a business trip the very last thing you want to do at the end of a day's driving is go twenty miles up into the hills to dine where George Washington (or Jesse James) once slept.

This means that you are limited to restaurants or cafeterias on, or immediately off, the freeway. Those at service areas are usually regulated by the state highway commission. Those clustered at exits are either truck stops or chain restaurants like Howard Johnson's, Denny's, or Victoria Station. On the outskirts of a large city you will find the fast-food "franchise row"—Burger King, Arthur Treacher's, Dairy Queen, Wendy's, and the ubiquitous McDonald's. They are usually all within sight of one another—for comfort, one assumes. In some parts of the country you will find regional chains, like Bob Evans and Dutch Pantry in the Midwest. These are a little bit different, but after the sixth or seventh time you have eaten in one, not different enough.

There are some good things to be said for fast-food restaurants, the major one being that they are *fast*. Also, the food is freshly prepared, and you know what you are getting; there are no unpleasant surprises. No pleasant ones, either, of course.

I have a cousin who once drove from California to New York in three days. His strategy was to stop only once every eight hours. He would pull into a gas station and get the fill-up started, rush into the restaurant and order a couple of hamburgers and coffee to go, visit the men's room and pay for the gas while the food was being prepared, dash back to pick up his food, get in the car and go. It was a Volkswagen too. This no-sleep driving is *not* recommended, but the point is that if you are pushing to make time, you will not starve even if you never get more than fifty yards from the freeway.

One of the problems with this type of eating is that you are virtually limited to carbohydrates and protein. The only fresh vegetables are in preprepared and very tired-looking salads, and the only fruit is the canned variety, sitting there in sad little cups. Hot vegetables have been on the steam table for so long that you would get more nutritional value by eating your paper napkin. There are a few exceptions, but they are remarkable. At a truck stop in Indiana once, I went to pay my bill and found at the cashier's desk a large basket full of shiny red apples. They looked so good I almost cried. You can almost always get fruit juice though, which will at least keep your teeth from falling out.

Tables 1 and 2 on pages 106–7 give details of meal combinations at two of the largest fast-food chains, McDonald's and Burger King. These are items and combinations that work out to fewer than 400 calories per meal. Unless otherwise stated, it is assumed that your beverage is no-calorie soda or black coffee or tea. You could probably eat two such meals a day and stay healthy provided you got a couple of servings each of vegetables and fruit at the third meal (or had fresh fruit as a snack). If you were pregnant or nursing you would add more milk. Still, if I were going to try that kind of a diet for more than a few days I'd want to take a multivitamin pill each day.

TABLE 1: McDONALD'S

Meal	Calories	Grams Protein	Grams Carbohydrate
Egg McMuffin	350	18	26
Scrambled eggs and pork sausage	340	21	2
Scrambled eggs and buttered English muffin	350	18	30
Scrambled eggs and small order french fries	370	15	28
Scrambled eggs and orange juice	240	13	22
Scrambled eggs, orange juice, and milk	400	21	34
Pork sausage and small order french fries	390	12	26
Pork sausage and buttered English muffin	370	15	28
Buttered English muffin and orange juice	270	7	48
Dry English muffin, orange juice, and milk	400	15	60
Hamburger	260	13	30
Hamburger and orange juice	340	14	50
Hamburger and milk (discard half the roll)	370	21	30
Hamburger and small order french fries (discard all the roll)	370	16	26
Cheeseburger	300	16	31

Meal	Calories	Grams Protein	Carbohydrate
Cheeseburger and orange juice	380	17	51
Quarter-Pounder (discard half the roll)	370	26	20
Filet-o-Fish	400	14	34
Filet-o-Fish and orange juice (discard half the roll and scrape off half the tartar sauce)	400	15	54

Data courtesy McDonald's Corporation

TABLE 2: BURGER KING

Meal	Calories	Grams Protein	Grams Carbohydrate
Hamburger	240	13	25
Hamburger and small order french fries (discard half the roll)	390	16	25
Hamburger and small order onion rings	390	15	45
Double meat hamburger	370	25	25
Cheeseburger	310	17	26
Whopper Jr.	300	13	16
Whopper Jr. with cheese	350	17	26
Hot dog	290	11	24

Data courtesy Burger King Corporation

I wasn't able to put together low-calorie menus from the Kentucky Fried Chicken menu, but the data in Table 3 on page 108 will give you an idea of what you're getting. If you're on a high-protein, low-carbohydrate diet you would do all right with just the individual pieces of chicken, especially if you picked off some of the breading.

TABLE 3: KENTUCKY FRIED CHICKEN

One Dinner— three pieces of chicken, mashed potatoes and gravy, cole slaw and roll	Calories	Grams Protein	Grams Carbohydrate
Original Recipe	830	52	56
Extra Crispy	959	52	63
Individual Pieces—Original Recipe			
Wing	151	11	4
Drumstick	136	14	2
Keel	283	25	6
Rib	241	19	8
Thigh	276	20	12

Data courtesy International Food Service Co., Inc., and Heublein Food Service & Franchising Group

Let's say you eat breakfast and lunch at fast-food places and keep it under 400 calories per meal. Add 200 calories for a couple of pieces of fresh fruit while you're driving. (Apples and bananas are best because they won't drip all over your lap.) That's 1,000 calories, and leaves you another 1,000 for a decent dinner or three stiff drinks when you stop for the night. If you're trying to lose weight, you'd keep your dinner to 400 calories too—say, a large salad with hard-boiled egg or shrimp; or a piece of broiled chicken and a couple of diet-type vegetables. No matter how tired you are, driving is *not* hard physical labor. Don't kid yourself that you've had a lot of exercise just because your muscles hurt. You've been sitting down all day, so eat accordingly.

A note about french fried potatoes: it is always assumed that french fries are nutritionally useless and an absolute no-no in a reducing diet. In fact, a small order of, say, McDonald's french fries has fewer calories than a hamburger and about the same amount of fat. It has *less* fat than a cheeseburger. Also, that serving will give you about 20 percent of your daily requirement of vitamin C, which is not to be sniffed at when fresh fruit is hard to come by. This is not a license to eat unlimited quantities of french fries though; but once in a while you could throw away the hamburger roll and satisfy your craving for french fries instead without dropping dead on the spot.

A final word about fast-food eating: order the food to go and take it to your car to eat. This not only saves time, which is the whole point of the exercise, but it prevents you from going back for a milk shake or dessert. One shake, all by itself, has between 300 and 400 calories, depending on the flavor, and up to 60 grams of carbohydrate. And the McDonald's fruit pies, in case you never noticed, are *fried*. Each one has 300 calories and about twice as much fat as a hamburger.

The Traveling Gourmet

Business travel is a wonderful way to indulge your gourmet tendencies and become an amateur expert on regional cooking. On an expense account, or if you're the business guest of local people, the cost is not a primary consideration. You can go to the area's specialty restaurants and enjoy the items for which the region is well known. There's usually a good reason for their fame.

In this way you can get to try fresh salmon baked over coals in the Pacific Northwest, French Creole cooking in New Orleans, and Maine lobster and Indian pudding in New England. It's not difficult to track down the best places; you will probably have names and addresses of restaurants forced on you by proud local citizens.

I know a few people who collect recipes in restaurants, asking for the chef's specialty. I am a little doubtful about this. I once heard a story about a woman who asked for a recipe and was told by the chef that he would mail it to her. He did, along with a bill for $300. She protested loudly, but her lawyer told her to shut up and pay it. The man was a professional chef and recipes were his stock in trade. Whether or not the story is true, it seems to me that if you're that much of an avid cook, you can put together a reasonable facsimile of any dish at home, provided you can get the ingredients. There are thousands of cookbooks with regional specialties, and some even have lists of shops where you can get unusual ingredients. In many places you can find locally produced cookbooks featuring the region's special recipes. They make nice take-home presents for yourself, much better than a mug or an ashtray with the city's name on it.

Another nice thing to take home is the food. Some restaurants sell packaged versions of their best-known items, or you can visit the local supermarket or specialty food store. You'd pick items that travel reasonably well, of course. Cheese from Wisconsin; grits from the South (if you really like grits; I know many southerners who can't stand them either), also chicory coffee, cans of gumbo and okra, and other ingredients for Creole dishes; maple syrup and maple sugar products from New England; sourdough starter kits from San Francisco. In some places the airport shops feature a local item. For example, you can buy loaves of sourdough bread at San Francisco airport and live lobsters, packaged to travel, at Boston's Logan airport.

Enjoy.

7

"Table for One, Please"

This chapter is about doing things on your own, in non-business hours. One thing about travel is that, no matter how tough the day at work, you usually have more free time in the evenings than you would at home (no housework to do) and more unstructured time.

Doing things with someone else for company is often pleasant, of course. But the invitations from the business people you are visiting may run out; they can't spend every evening entertaining you. Colleagues you are traveling with may have things they want to do on their own. Anyway, it can get a little tiresome to spend all your free time with people you work with all day, no matter how well you get along together. Being willing and able to entertain yourself, by yourself, is one of the hallmarks of an independent person.

In this chapter I'll discuss some of the things you might find to do away from home, give some suggestions for how to find them, and talk a little about the style in which to do them. The diversity of human interests being what it is, however, I can make no attempt to be comprehensive. Your special thing might be betting on the horses, or playing all-night poker. If I really thought about it I might be able to come up with some tips for how to have yourself recommended to the local bookie or the most likely places to find the perpetual floating table-stakes game. Because I can't cover everything, you'll have to take the guidelines given and apply them to your own lifestyle.

Finding the Action

Unless you are inordinately travel-shy, you will find more than enough interesting things to do in a large city. Guidebooks, tourist magazines given away in the large hotels, and the entertainment section of the local Sunday paper will provide you with more than enough ideas, no matter what your interests. Also, try the local "underground" or alternative newspaper, usually a weekly. In New York, it's the *Village Voice,* of course; Boston has both the *Real Paper* and the *Phoenix*; San Francisco's come and go, but at last check it was the *Bay Guardian.* Most other large cities have their equivalents. Even if you don't find entertainment possibilities not listed in the establishment publications, you'll at least get a somewhat different view of the life of the city.

Asking a few of the people in the office will provide you with another long list. Most people want to show off their city to visitors. You will get tips on undiscovered restaurants, neighborhood art shows, places to stay away from because they're too mobbed with tourists, and perhaps even how to score for dope, if that's what you want.

A few phone calls before you leave will also get you names of restaurants and names of people to look up. "I'm going to be spending a couple of weeks in ———. Who do you know there?" You'll garner everybody from old Aunt Minnie who lives forty miles out in the suburbs, to the most eligible bachelor in Columbus, Ohio. Everyone is worth at least a phone call when you get there, and you may spend some interesting evenings seeing a side of the city you would not otherwise have discovered.

The situation is a little different in smaller communities, especially if there is no large city within, say, an hour's drive, making it reasonably accessible for an evening out. But even very small towns often have at least one natural wonder, famous institution, historical personage, or other attraction that the Chamber of Commerce can boast of. Don't scorn these. They must have some value to someone, or they wouldn't have become notable. You will probably find they are more interesting than they sounded, and at the very least, you will learn something new, and what have you got to lose? A few hours of sitting in your motel room contemplating the wallpaper?

On this principle I have become a minor expert on such things as the local artists' colony in Toledo, the sex habits of salmon, Australian opals, the cavern-dwelling proclivities of the Olentangy Indians, soul food restaurants in Beloit, Wisconsin, and New Hampshire's Hannah Dustin, who was captured by marauding Indians and at the first opportunity killed and scalped the lot of them, thus becoming an example to us all. To name but a few.

You can use your trips to advance a hobby, trace your ancestors, enhance a collection, or build a small but respectable library of specialty books. For example, if you are a Civil War buff, raging or incipient, you are within striking distance of a battlefield or other notable site almost anywhere in the eastern half of the country. Or you may discover a new interest, or something to follow up on your next trip.

I once bought a very nice piece of sculpture in Seattle, but it took two trips to do it. I couldn't afford it the first time, so I left a deposit and spent the next six months saving to redeem my treasure on the second trip. It was well worth it. Or, another example: I discovered two monuments to Hannah Dustin, one in Penacook on the site of her revengeful deed, and another in Nashua at the house where she sought refuge after her escape. These are separated by what is now a good hour's drive on the freeway. How on earth did she get there? Not on foot, if the dates and times on the stone markers are correct. Did she steal a horse? Did she go by boat down a river? And why did she travel so far before knocking on someone's door . . . were there no other doors in between in those days? These questions have been bothering me sorely, and I intend to get answers next time I'm back in that part of the country.

Geography

A special word here for native easterners: try to overcome, or at least hide, your provincialism. Most easterners (and I am one of them) are brought up to believe that everything between Philadelphia and the Rockies is a giant dustbowl, literally and figuratively. It's just not true. There are real people out there doing real things just like the rest of us. I have never once seen a coonskin hat or failed to find a bar of soap in the local supermarket. A hundred years ago there may have been striking differences for the traveler to complain about, but today you will find people just as fashionably dressed in downtown Cleveland as on Fifth Avenue, a bartender in Louisville will mix you a Rusty Nail without raising an eyebrow, and there are people in Lansing who have actually heard of Truman Capote.

It is true that the more one knows about a subject, the more interesting it becomes. When I first started traveling in the Midwest, I wished I had paid more attention in my high school geography and history classes. There is an indefinable thrill at seeing the Rockies for the first time, realizing that your route parallels the trail taken by the Donner party, or discovering you are about to cross the Great Divide. After you have driven over your hundredth set of train tracks in a day, the fact that the opening of the West depended on railroads takes on new significance.

Rivers are very interesting too. I was once driving along somewhere in the Midwest, not even sure of which state I was in, thinking more about making it to my stop for the night than about the local scenery, when I realized I was crossing a river. Had been crossing it for some time, in fact. I've seen a lot of rivers, including the Hudson, the Charles, the Thames, the Seine, and the Rhine, but this one was the grandmother and the grandfather of them all. I knew it wasn't the Mississippi, I'd crossed that the day before and had not been impressed. The damn thing just went on and on, and finally, after what seemed several miles, I got to the far side and saw the small sign: Missouri River. The Great Missouri. I spent the rest of the day laughing to myself (and at myself) and inappropriately humming Stephen Foster songs.

I suppose that westerners have similar revelations upon visiting Revolutionary War sites for the first time, or on viewing Plymouth Rock.

Another "collection" to build is that of global demarcations. Crossing the equator for the first time is supposed to be the premier such experience, but I did it in the air, with no ceremony. Still, it was something to talk about. Less dramatic but no less interesting are crossing the International Date Line and crossing the latitude line that is exactly halfway between the equator and the

North Pole—I did it in Oregon and never would have known it except that some kindly soul had put up a marker on the freeway. My favorite, though, is being at zero longitude, in Greenwich, England. You can stand with one foot in the eastern hemisphere and one foot in the western hemisphere.

One at a Time

Now we come to the question of going to public places alone. In particular, this means restaurants and movie theaters—I don't know any woman who feels uncomfortable going to a shopping mall by herself, for example, or to the hairdresser's. (If these do worry you, you probably need psychological help.)

But restaurants and movies pose special difficulties. By being alone in these places you automatically signal to every weirdo, freak, and unattached male within fifty miles that you are "available," and it doesn't matter to them how you might feel about it. In their eyes you're fair game.

I know several women who travel a great deal and who will *never* sit down alone in a restaurant. For breakfast and lunch they stop at fast-food restaurants and eat in the car, and they get dinner from room service at the hotel. The only time they eat "out" is with other people. I have discussed this with them at length because it is difficult for me to understand; I like eating alone in a restaurant. They cite two reasons: the first I've already mentioned, the problem of what to do about men on the make. They find it uncomfortable to ignore and would rather eat in their rooms than have the hassle. The second reason is social: they seem to feel that they will be seen as undesirable because they are not escorted by a man. My attitude is just the opposite and, I think, more liberated. I like advertising the fact that I'm independent and that I can damn well afford to pay for my own meals. Or that I have a job that includes a liberal expense account, as the case may be.

I am not usually bothered by men either, unless I want to be (picking up men in public places is discussed in another chapter).

I think that one's attitude has something to do with it. I walk in confidently and say, "Dinner for one, please," or whatever is appropriate. Very often, the hostess or maitre d' is busy looking around behind me to see who I'm with; I just ignore this. I avoid eye contact with the other diners, and that seems to close the door for all but the drunks. I have never, to my knowledge, been deliberately given the draftiest table or the one right beside the kitchen door, just because I was a woman alone. I will admit that there have been occasions when the service was so slow or so rude that I demanded the check and walked out without finishing, but I have no way of knowing whether this would have happened anyway, even if I'd been with Robert Redford.

The key is to act as if you belong there and deserve just as good service as everyone else is getting, even if you have to hype yourself up psychologically the first few times. You *do* belong there and *are* entitled to good service.

And if the service is good, leave a decent tip. I get a perverse pleasure out of seeing the waiter do a double-take when he sees a 15 or 20 percent tip. Although I have no figures to back it up, I do not believe that women tip worse than men. But your waiter believes they do and has been mentally preparing himself for a little pile of pennies and nickels. Drop that dollar bill (or two) down and walk away without looking back. And do make it folding money rather than change. Somehow, it is more psychologically satisfying to pick up a dollar bill than four quarters. Get rid of your change somewhere else, say, at the cash register where they will appreciate having it.

I have seen men leave dreadful tips. The most memorable occasion was when the general manager of one of our divisions took me out to lunch. I knew that this man's salary was about $60,000 a year. The check came to $32 and of course it was going to go on his expense account. He paid with a fifty-dollar bill, and left a tip of $2, less than 7 percent. The service had been extremely prompt and cheerful, and I felt so dreadful that I would have slipped more money onto the tray if I could have done it without having the G.M. notice.

When you are eating alone, there is one special consideration: there is no such thing as a table for one. At the very least, you are occupying a table for two. If your waiter had served two people, the check (on the average) would have been twice as much, and his tip would have been twice as big. So, especially if you dawdle over your meal and are depriving him of an extra "turnover" on the table, keep this in mind when calculating your tip.

Movies present a slightly different problem. It's dark, and you may be in close physical proximity to those around you. You probably already know the basic rules for what to do about the hand on your knee or the flasher. Get up and move. Leave, if it's that bad. Complain to the management. Even so, your evening has been spoiled. (I know of one exception to this. A young cousin of mine, a teenager, was once visiting me. She went off on her own to see a movie and came home bubbling with laughter. A man had sat next to her and exposed himself. "It's happened to all my friends," she said, "on buses, on the street, in movies. I was beginning to worry that something was wrong with me because I'd never had the experience. Now I have.")

If you go to an "adult" movie house by yourself, you are asking for it, of course. Maybe that's why you're there, and if so, I'll assume you're ready for whatever happens. In more legitimate circumstances, however, you have to make a reasoned decision on whether it's worth the risk of having your entertainment ruined.

Many women I know have decided against it and just don't go to a movie alone. If they can't round up a companion, they do something else. I would prefer to have company too, but once in a while there's a film I really want to see and everyone else has seen it, or they have got other plans, so I go alone. You can make your own decision.

Music and Theater

Live theater productions and concerts are a different story. I am a theater aficionado and always try to catch local productions that sound promising. I know women who feel the same about recitals and concerts, and on comparing notes with them, I find that we agree that this can be done without any hassle. I guess it's just that the type of audience attracted to these events is of a different nature, or at least, they have different standards of behavior than do moviegoers. In fact, you get into some interesting conversations during intermissions, having a very handy subject to open with, and there's always the possibility you'll meet someone you want to see again. I don't go with this idea in mind, but it has happened.

A friend of mine went to see a play in England. During the intermission, in the women's room, she saw an older woman who looked very familiar. My friend talked with her for a few minutes about the play, trying to puzzle out where they had met before. But she couldn't remember and so didn't say anything else. It wasn't until the next day that she realized the woman she had talked with was the Queen Mother.

Even if you don't get to chat with royalty, theatrical and musical events are very safe bets for a woman alone. I would imagine that the same is true of opera, but that's not one of my interests. If it is yours, you'll know how to choose what to see and what the appropriate standards of conduct and attire are.

If you hunger for a different kind of music—disco, rock, jazz, blue-grass, country-and-western, folk—you'll need to find out about local nightclubs and discos. The possibilities vary widely in different cities. San Francisco is paradise for a woman alone. I found a half-dozen clubs where I could go by myself, have a drink and catch the act, and feel perfectly comfortable about it. New York and Boston aren't bad either, provided you stay away from the more notorious singles bars. Other cities range from hopeless to pretty good. (I'm not going to recommend any particular places because the club may have closed or the ambience changed since I was there.)

The way to find good places to go alone is to ask. Choose single people at the office in the city you're visiting, or those you know who are familiar with the city. It's interesting to analyze the kinds of answers you get; they sometimes reveal a lot about the person you're talking to. Some men, even, are quite sensitive about the problems a woman alone might have, and will have very definite suggestions for places where you'll feel comfortable and those where you won't. It seems to depend not on the type of music or on the renown of the club, or even on its geographical location. The difference seems to be in the atmosphere the management has created and the types of people that patronize the place.

In Seattle, for example, I had accumulated a short list of discos and jazz clubs, and asked several people their advice about which ones would be suitable for me to go to alone. One disco was singled out as *the* place to stay away from; even though it was a "classy joint," a woman alone would inevitably be hassled. Others were rated as OK or so-so. I stayed away from that one place, but did try a few of the others, and the advice I'd been given proved to be very accurate.

I've found that I can judge fairly quickly whether the establishment is one I'm going to feel comfortable in. My suggestion, if you want to try this kind of thing, is to go the first time on a weekday evening, for the early show. (Call to find out.) I usually avoid places that have an admission or cover charge on weekday evenings, because if it turns out to be a bummer I'll be leaving in a few minutes and will have wasted the money.

When you walk in the door, pause for a moment and make a quick judgment. If there's no one at the bar except single men, all without ties and drinking beer, turn around and walk right out again. A lot of shouting and carrying on is bad news too. At the best, you won't be able to hear the music. If it's all singles, it might be strictly a pick-up joint. If the women are wearing black net stockings and hot pants, you're probably not going to feel comfortable there. The best sign is a combined clientele: some groups of men together, some groups of women together, some singles. A place like that is apt to be very relaxed and hassle-free. Racially mixed places are always good bets too.

I always sit at the bar, at least the first time. At a table alone you're momentarily trapped if some klutz sits down without being invited. At the bar you can always turn to look the other way to end an approach, or go to the women's room and take a different seat when you come back. I usually chat with the bartender for a moment, if he's not too busy, so I feel I have a "friend" if I need one. More than once this has been useful, when a man I didn't want to talk to wouldn't give up trying. The bartender caught on to what was happening and spent enough time polishing the bar in our territory, scowling, to get the message through to the interloper. Another trick, if you don't want to look like you're expecting a pick-up, is to turn to other customers to include them in the conversation. I've started some interesting discussions this way. And, of course, once the music starts you can concentrate on that and make it clear you don't want to talk.

When you find a place you like, make a note of it for the next time you're back. If the bartender and the other employees get to know you, you'll feel like a regular and will be sure of enjoying yourself. I'm a little cautious when returning to a place on a weekend night, though; I find that the atmosphere is often different from what it was during the week.

Reading

Now for a change of pace, from nightclubs to reading. If you like to read, you'll find yourself doing a lot of it on a business trip. You may need to spread out your papers and do some work on the plane, which is very impressive, but after you finish that the best thing to do to escape boredom on a plane is to read. The airline always has a supply of the latest magazines, and I find this a good way to catch up on publications I wouldn't ordinarily buy or subscribe to.

Many people, including myself, wouldn't dream of starting out on a business trip without one or two paperbacks stuck in their briefcases. My preference is light reading, best-selling novels and thrillers. They're not too much work and are often very entertaining—that's how they got to be best-sellers.

My problem is that I read so much I can end up after a two-week trip with twenty pounds of books to lug back home. Sometimes I give them away or leave them in the hotel room.

I dislike throwing away books, though. On longer trips, the solution is the public library. I have found that you can always get a temporary nonresident's card. The procedure varies and you may find that the staff are stumped when you first ask. But it's almost impossible for a true librarian to deny a person who obviously wants to read books. Sometimes they issue a free temporary card; sometimes you have to pay a small fee; sometimes the rule is that you have to leave a deposit equal to the price of the books. At times, I've had $40 or $50 on semipermanent deposit at the local library. But you do get it back when you return the books.

Some travelers feel uncomfortable reading in a restaurant. I'm not one of them, provided there's enough light. If you're self-conscious about pulling out your paperback, you might feel better with a magazine or the local newspaper.

For an avid reader, getting stuck somewhere without

something to read can be a disaster. I'll read myself to sleep with the room-service menu if there's nothing else. I was once on a train in northern France with a colleague. Something went wrong and we just sat in the middle of nowhere for four hours. We finished our paperbacks and started looking for something else to read. We began to unload our pockets, briefcases, and handbags. It's amazing how engrossing the back of a ticket stub or the stamps in someone else's passport can be when you're desperate. On another occasion, I was with a business partner at London's Heathrow airport. Our plane was delayed, but we'd already checked through Immigration and couldn't return to the main terminal. There was one small shop with a very limited choice of reading matter. We bought a book that listed outrageous one-line insults in five languages and spent a glorious hour taking turns reading it to each other. I guess it was the circumstances, but the more we read the funnier it got. Our fellow passengers thought we were crazy, sitting there reading out insults and laughing like loons.

Having something interesting to read can be a lifesaver when you're alone. It's an activity that you can do anywhere, and if you're still shy about going to public places by yourself, you can stay in and read.

I suppose I should say something about TV too. The truth is that I rarely watch it, but I guess it's as acceptable an activity as reading when you're alone. I always feel better about it if I've taken along some embroidery or other handwork; to me it seems slothful to be doing nothing while I'm watching TV.

Other Activities

As I said at the beginning of this chapter, I've made no attempt to be comprehensive. There are so many interesting things to do during your free time in a new place that the problem may only be in choosing.

I wanted to include something about swinging. For the uninitiated, that means orgies, partner-swapping, and other group sex activities. I gather, from my somewhat limited research, that there's a great deal of it going on out there. I asked several people I know who make that scene from time to time. They said that if that's what you want, the best way to make contact with like-minded people is through the personal ads in the underground newspapers and swingers' magazines. You can usually find these at the local bookstore that specializes in dirty books . . . or, as they're euphemistically called, adult books. I visited a couple of bookstores of that type, at first with some trepidation, but I found the staff very friendly and the other customers just as anxious to keep their business to themselves as I was. Look in the local Yellow Pages under bookstores for the ones that say "adult books."

I haven't mentioned sports activities because I'm going to talk about that in the next chapter. And Chapter 9 includes suggestions for meeting men.

8
Health

This chapter assumes that you're in reasonably good health and want to stay that way. Feeling crummy is bad enough, but somehow it's much crummier when you're on the road. Furthermore, being away from home is a strain in itself, even without the possible added stress of business dealings with people you don't know in strange surroundings. Most of the suggestions given here, accumulated from my own experience and that of others, are just common sense, but there are some ideas you might not have thought of. I'm not going to discuss such special problems as physical handicaps or severe psychiatric conditions, having neither the expertise nor the experience to do so.

The basic idea, of course, is a sound mind in a sound

body. These are closely linked to each other. A basic requisite for both is eating right, which I've dealt with in a previous chapter. I'll therefore skip that now and concentrate on other key issues.

Sleep

The important thing about sleep is to get enough of it. How much that is varies from one person to another, and you know what it is for yourself. I find that when I'm traveling I function better if I get a little more than I do at home. For me, that means eight and a half to nine hours a night, as opposed to seven and a half to eight. That would seem excessive to some people, though. You can experiment and find out for yourself what your best level is.

I've noticed that some women push themselves much harder than a man would in a similar situation, trying for long travel hours and being bright and early at work the next morning with not enough sleep. I suppose it's the we-have-to-be-better-to-stay-in-the-same-place syndrome. I stopped doing it when I noticed that the men in the office automatically planned their travel for business hours or took an extra day to get there. Why should I work a full day and then travel all evening if they didn't? Now I leave from the office at noon.

Most modern motels and hotels have reasonably good mattresses, so that is rarely a problem. I almost always have to ask for an extra blanket, though, or if there are two beds in the room I'll just double up the blankets. I like to sleep in a cool room, and I particularly dislike not being able to open a window.

If you have trouble sleeping away from home, there are two options. One is to just lie awake for several nights, till you get so tired that you become "acclimated." Most people I know who had trouble sleeping in strange places when they first started traveling soon got over it, and can now sleep anywhere. If this doesn't seem to be happening to you, you could consider asking your doctor for a mild sleeping pill or tranquilizer.

In this connection there is one advantage to being female. I find it much easier to leave a party early or to beg off an evening altogether when I'm tired. Men traveling together in groups seem to feel that they have to keep up with each other. They would somehow lose face if they left before the bar closed. I just excuse myself early and it seems to be accepted. Next morning I'm the only one who's had a good night's sleep and isn't hung over.

Exercise

If you're used to exercising regularly, you know that you start to feel the lack of it if you've been away from home for a while. It can be difficult to keep up your routine. Any sport that requires equipment may present a problem. You don't always want to take your golf clubs or your tennis racket with you. Also, any sport that requires a partner may not be practicable on trips; similarly, finding the right setting—court, greens—is not always possible.

If you're really sports-addicted, you'll find ways and means wherever you are, though. I know one accountant who had to spend a month in the middle of the mountains of Oregon, with no recreational facilities within a radius of fifty miles. He was staying in a cabin in the woods. The cabin, however, had an old basketball hoop over the front door. At the first opportunity, he went into town and bought a basketball, and shot baskets for an hour every evening. Says he got pretty good at it too. When you have a lemon, make lemonade.

The best activities for someone who travels a lot are those that can be done alone and which require little or no equipment. Closest to the ideal in these respects are probably jogging, swimming, and calisthenics. They require only the right clothing, and not even that for calisthenics you do in your room.

I know some confirmed joggers who claim their exercise can be carried out anywhere. I am a little doubtful about the truth of this. First of all, you need to find an appropriate road or track. Second, there are some areas you might be in where you're not sure if it would be safe to be out there alone early in the morning or in late evening. Still, joggers seem to be able to carry on anywhere.

Swimming is pretty good because so many large motels have indoor pools nowadays. This doesn't work if the place is filled with tourists and families, though. It's impossible to do serious swimming in a pool full of kids.

I've always wished they had adults' times and children's times, but I've never seen a place that did. Another drawback is that those pools are so heavily chlorinated. I find that after twenty minutes of steady swimming, which is the minimum for a decent workout, my eyes have filmed over from the chlorine in the water. Not to mention what it does to your hair.

If you're one of those people who can get down on the floor and just exercise for a half-hour, that's the easiest solution. It doesn't take any equipment, you can do it in your room (maybe after rearranging the furniture a little), and you can set your own schedule.

I like this type of exercise but have difficulty maintaining a routine. One of the smartest things I did when I began to travel virtually full-time was to join a health club. I recommend this for anyone. Be sure that the club belongs to a group called the International Physical Fitness Association. Most Vic Tanneys are in this group, for example, as well as many other health clubs. They publish a national directory of several hundred associated clubs. Every large city has at least one, and many cities have half a dozen. If you belong to one, you can use the facilities at any other as a visitor without paying an additional charge. The facilities usually include exercise equipment, sauna, steam room, Jacuzzi (whirlpool), and sometimes a sun room for tanning and a swimming pool.

If you don't already belong and are considering this, shop around in your home city. Your membership fee is what's charged by your home club, and every club has different deals. If you are joining primarily to get out-of-town privileges, the location and the luxury of the facilities of your home club may be of less concern than getting the cheapest possible membership. Take into account the annual renewal fee too, which is considerably less than the original membership. All clubs will give you a free trial visit, which will usually include a high-powered sales pitch to get you to sign on the spot. Resist until you've checked out all the possibilities; even if you're told "This is a special deal for this week only," don't be rushed. You will very likely be offered the same special deal two weeks later.

I find that I tend to use the clubs even more when out of town than I do when at home. It's fun to compare their approaches to exercise (an instructor in one club will tell you that sit-ups are very bad for you, while it's the most praised routine in another) and the facilities. Some have opulent saunas and sun rooms, others have interesting new exercise machines to try out. All these clubs have regular free classes for group exercising. I find that I am much more likely to actually do forty-five minutes of hard work when I've gone to a club and changed into tights and leotard. I might start the routine in my hotel room, but then get interrupted or bored and do only ten minutes.

Besides exercise tights and leotard, you'll need a towel, which can be borrowed from your hotel room. And you'll probably want a bathing suit for the sauna and whirlpool. In some states a bathing suit is required in the pools, in others there's no law, but local custom dictates a suit. A few clubs are coed. I take along a five-year-old bikini, what the hell. And one final item: a combination lock for your locker. I carry everything in a small canvas tote bag that goes in my suitcase.

A further advantage of belonging to an association is that when you're alone in a strange city, it gives you somewhere to head to after work instead of just back to your hotel, and you can be sure of being welcome. I was once on a long trip by road, and hadn't had anyone say anything nice to me for three days except for a service station attendant, who then short-changed me. I was going through Louisville, Kentucky (where I knew no one), in the middle of the afternoon and stopped and looked up the local club in my directory. I went there and had a long exercise session, sauna, and swim—the place had excellent facilities—and talked with some of the staff. When I started driving again I was in a much better frame of mind.

Mental Health

Many people suffer from mild depression, lonesomeness, and symptoms of stress when they're on long trips. This can be true even if you have business colleagues for companionship in the evening and on weekends as well as on the job. No matter how well acquainted you are with people you work with, you can never relax as fully with them as you would with close personal friends and family. Being separated from people you love and who love you often causes stress, even if very mild.

The first thing you can do is to keep in touch, the way Ma Bell encourages you to. Most companies are reasonable about letting you put a certain amount on your expense account for calls home. If the operating unit you are visiting has a tie-line or WATS line to your home base, they are usually quite agreeable about letting you use it. At some locations I visit regularly, out-of-town business visitors get unlimited use of the tie-line outside of business hours, a nice fringe benefit. Even if you have to pay for it yourself, it's worth it. Except if you do what one man I know did: he fell asleep while talking long-distance to his family in New Orleans and had to pay for a three-hour call. Another story: I was once talking long-distance with a friend who was out of town, and *he* fell asleep in the bathtub. Fearing he had drowned, I hung up and called the hotel manager to go up and rescue him. They had to break down the door and found him snoring, with the phone under water.

Spending some of your free time shopping for presents to take back home is a morale-booster too.

Exercise combats mild depression. So does keeping busy. It can be a letdown to spend a frantic day working and then get back to the hotel and find yourself wondering what to do. You don't have the normal chores you would at home, there's more unstructured time. It helps if you plan something, even if it's only a long bath and something in particular on TV. You could use some of the free time to pay more attention to your grooming. I find that the manicures I give myself are never better than when I'm on the road.

In the last chapter, I discussed other activities and gave suggestions for ways and means of going about them. Remember, though, not to overdo the social activities to the detriment of your sleeping time.

Many people solve the lonesomeness problem, at least partially, by talking to strangers. Being a New Englander, I find it difficult to confide in a stranger, but I can see the advantage. If it's someone you'll never see again, it doesn't matter what you say about your personal life. I guess this is the reason why bartenders have a reputation for being good listeners and amateur psychiatrists.

As a last resort, you could always go home. One woman I talked with when I was preparing this book told how she once got so lonesome that she did exactly that. She is black, which is relevant to the story. She was assigned to spend several weeks at a company site halfway across the country from her home, in a small town. She said that the local population was 100 percent white, and although there weren't any racial problems, she had no one to talk to and she just felt uncomfortable being stared at everywhere she went. On Friday afternoon she impulsively drove to the airport, and got a flight home for the weekend, returning on Sunday night. "It cost a couple of hundred dollars altogether," she said, "but it saved my sanity in that place and I never regretted spending the money."

Menstruation

I have read in a number of sources that female flight attendants, especially those who travel east-west and west-east distances over time zones, often have problems with their periods. However, none of the women I talked with in preparing this book mentioned their periods as a special difficulty.

Male doctors, on the other hand, worry about it all the time. An English doctor was recently quoted in the press as stating that a woman should not drive during the eight days before and after her period, because of reduced vision and impaired reflexes. It wasn't clear if he meant eight days a month altogether, or eight days before and eight after. He seems to have the worrying under control, so I'll just let him keep on with it and not take it upon myself.

If you have a severe problem with cramps or premenstrual tension, you might need medical attention anyway, whether or not you travel.

Emergencies

It's miserable to be away from home and get sick. I've had it happen a number of times. I, and several others with me, once had food poisoning in Australia. I was so sick it got past the point where I was afraid I was going to die, and I started being afraid I *wasn't* going to die. At that point (it was 3 A.M.) I did what I should have done earlier, which was to call the front desk and ask for the doctor. It turned out he was already in the hotel treating one of the others, and within ten minutes he'd confirmed my diagnosis and given me an injection. Another time, in

Seattle, I caught some kind of intestinal bug that was never precisely diagnosed but was causing such pain that I would have suspected appendicitis, except that I'd had an emergency appendectomy three years before in England. In Seattle, I went to the nearest hospital emergency room. Antibiotics cleared that up in a few days.

You know the signs of a real problem: any kind of bad pain, unusual bleeding, fever. Don't be a martyr—get help. Every hotel has a local doctor they can call for you. I've never heard of a request for a doctor *not* getting very prompt action. The last thing a hotel wants is to find, excuse the expression, a stiff in one of their rooms. Or go to the nearest hospital emergency room, even if it's something you'd ordinarily just call your family doctor about back home. Tell them you're from out of town. If you have group medical insurance through your company, always carry the card.

It's a good idea, too, to carry in your wallet a card specifying your blood type and any allergies you have, and anything else that should be known if you're unconscious—for example, that you wear contact lenses. Also, an organ donor card, if that's your preference. Some states now put organ donor statements on the driver's license.

Most cities have an emergency service for severe toothache or other emergency dental problems. Check the phone book. Failing that, go to a dentist's office and collapse.

If you're not sick enough for a doctor or the hospital but still are indisputably ill, use the same judgment about whether to go to work that you would at home. Stay in your hotel room and throw yourself on the mercy of room service for hot tea and soup. Having said that, I realize that I don't always follow my own advice. I knew I was coming down with the flu a few months ago, but undertook an overnight trip to one of our plants anyway. I felt so awful I doubt I contributed anything useful. The worst times were the takeoffs and landings—twelve of them in twenty-four hours—because it hurt my ears so much. It was another three days before the ear aches stopped.

Sex

That certainly belongs in this chapter. Masturbate, take a friend with you, do without, or find it where you can. The next chapter gives suggestions for the last alternative.

9

Men

Lots of them. Pastures of plenty, out there in the friendly skies and in the cocktail lounges of America's innkeepers.

When I was checking out the United Airlines statistics I quoted earlier, their representative wrote to me that women travelers have increased "a dramatic 54 percent over the same period last year." That is, up from 16 percent of business travelers to 18 percent. (Want to try that one again? It reads like a 2 percent increase to me, not 54 percent, but I guess United has its own way of looking at these things.) Anyway, it still says that more than 80 percent are male. Or to put it another way, four of them for each one of us.

For starters, we can divide all the men into two categories. There are those you would like to get to know better for personal reasons, and those you wouldn't. If you're happily married, then maybe all other men will be in the second category because you're just not interested. In that case you can skip the second half of this chapter.

For the men you want to keep at arm's length, we can further divide them into those you work with and those you don't. It is my opinion that two of these groups should be identical—that is, the men you work with should *always* be in the category of those you don't want a sexual relationship with. There may be some exceptions or special situations, but they are few, and fewer still result in a happy ending.

On Not Mixing Business With Pleasure

It's an old truism that it's a bad idea to have an affair with someone you work with. This is especially true if the man is your boss. It's even truer if he's married and you're single. This is disastrous. I've seen not just careers but whole lives wrecked by that. I managed to avoid it by luck for the first ten years of my working life, and by that time I was too smart to let it happen. I hope you never let it happen either.

Many such liaisons start on business trips. You're both away from home; the opportunity is right smack in front of you. You're strangers in the city you're visiting, so feelings of camaraderie and closeness between you grow quickly. Over a good expense-account dinner in a dimly lighted restaurant, with wine and after-dinner brandy, you finish discussing the client or the meeting and begin to talk about personal matters. What happens next is that you go to your room or his, for a nightcap. That's one step too far.

If you're afraid you might be vulnerable, don't let even the first step happen. Be sure that there's a crowd at dinner—invite the client and his wife and his whole family if you can, or any other business acquaintances you can round up. If that's impossible, invent relatives you have to visit because they'd never forgive you if they found out you'd been in their town and not stopped to see them; or as a last resort, plead fatigue or illness and have a room-service dinner. Put the chain on your door and don't answer the phone, if things are that bad.

These things are to protect you from yourself. A much more common situation will be one in which you have to protect *him* from *himself*. It's truly amazing how many happily married, church-going businessmen go completely bonkers the minute they get away from home for the night.

As before, the best cure is prevention. Stay in a crowd and avoid flirtations that, however innocent they may seem to you, may be accidentally or deliberately misunderstood. At the first sign of untoward behavior, take some action to end it right there. But above all, pretend it never happened; you'll save face for the man and you'll be able to work together next morning.

Here's an example of the kind of thing that happens over and over again. I was attending a convention with a number of other executives from my company, all male. We met for a pre-dinner drink in the hotel cocktail lounge. We were only halfway through the first drink when I felt a hand on my knee. The hand belonged to the divisional controller, a man I'd worked with before and known for a year. Our relationship had always been one-hundred-percent business, and I intended to keep it that way. I excused myself to go to the women's room, and by the time I returned others had joined the group, so I was able to take a different chair. But on the way out to dinner, the controller managed to walk beside me and put his arm around my waist. I had to do something, immediately. If I'd let it continue, the man would have made a fool out of himself in front of our colleagues, and that would have wrecked our future working relationship.

I picked another man in the group, one I knew well and had traveled with before. I knew he was cool and quick-witted, and would keep sober throughout the evening. Also, he was driving the rental car. In the confusion of going out the revolving door, I got him aside for a few seconds and said, "Greg, please stay between me and the controller, all night." He caught on immediately, as I knew he would, and winked and said "Gotcha, don't worry." He then gracefully arranged it so that I didn't sit next to the controller in the car or at dinner.

In other situations you may not have an ally to turn to. In that case, you just have to keep moving away, changing the conversation. Try not to have a confrontation—don't admit that anything unusual is going on, again for face-saving reasons. As a last resort only, speak straight and say, "I think we should keep this impersonal" or whatever is appropriate.

One difficulty is that the never-never-land atmosphere of being away from home, combined with alcohol, results in very rapidly deteriorating situations. You may have no warning at all before the lunge for your neckline or the knee between your legs in the hotel corridor. If you'd had any suspicions you would have avoided being in the hotel corridor alone with him in the first place. Now he's got you backed against the wall and is breathing gin fumes into your ear. What to do?

The first and no-exception rule is, *don't go into a hotel room with him*, yours or his. If you've already got the door to your room open and he's pushing his way in, *you leave*. If there's any other person in your group, go to the front desk and call—another man is the best choice—and say, "So-and-so isn't feeling very well, could you please help?" When you get back to your room you will probably find that so-and-so has left. At that point you can send the reinforcements back home. If he's still in your room, he may have passed out. Send in your ally to evaluate the situation. If necessary, take another room for the night. And remember the face-saving; in the morning, pretend nothing has happened, or at the worst that the man was a little indisposed. Leave it at that.

Let's go back to the gin-breathing dumbo in the hotel corridor. You can't use subtlety if it's gone that far. Use physical force to push him away and verbal communication to tell him to stop. If he's only a little drunk, your raised voice will probably be enough—the last thing he wants is embarrassment and that will bring him to his senses. If he's really falling-down drunk, you can probably defend yourself against him even if he's twice your size. Cause a commotion, get away from him, go to a hotel house phone to get help.

If you're not traveling with anyone else and have no ally to call on, in the worst situations you'll have to ask the hotel to send around their security person. This is a last resort, because once official action is taken the man has lost face. On the other hand, he may be so drunk that he won't remember the details in the morning, which lets you gloss it over and maintain some semblance of a good working relationship.

Turning Down Strangers

So far I've been talking about men you know and work with. Avoiding unwanted approaches from strangers is much easier because you can be blunt and don't have to worry about maintaining a business relationship. A simple "No, thanks" or, "Sorry, I'm busy" is usually sufficient. You don't need to give a reason or excuses.

One woman I know has a standard put-down line that always works. She says, "My husband wouldn't like it." This bothers me for two reasons. First of all, she isn't married. But even if she were, the statement implies that she has no mind of her own, that she's the property of a man who gives her no freedom to decide for herself whether she wants to talk to a stranger. This is a lot different from asking other men for help in difficult situations—there, you're taking the initiative yourself and using the resources at hand.

Some men become (or pretend to be) terribly offended by a refusal. I remember one evening when I'd been driving until midnight and just wanted a glass of wine in the hotel cocktail lounge before bed. I was exhausted and not interested in company. A man sat next to me in the bar and offered to buy me another drink. When I said no thanks, he acted as if he'd been mortally wounded. He couldn't believe I'd be so rude and unfeeling. After I'd repeated my refusal three times, he turned his bar stool so he was facing the wall and had his back to me and sat that way until I left. Crushed his manhood, bitchy me.

Some men, because they've had too much to drink or just because they're nerds, won't accept "no" and make pests of themselves. When it gets to the point where my enjoyment is ruined, I get up and leave. On rare occasions the man will follow you out. In that case I wouldn't head for my room, but would go to the hotel desk or some other public point where assistance would be at hand—for example, to an information counter, if the setting is an airport. If you haven't lost your company by then, ask for a security person, the manager, or someone else with authority. I've never had to go that far, but I would if I felt it was necessary.

At times the situation gets a little more tricky. I was at a seminar last year when one of the younger women in our group came to me for advice. She had been getting phone calls in her room from a man who had seen her.

He had apparently noted her room number and found out her name from the front desk. He kept calling to ask her for a date. Being a trusting and friendly person, at first she talked to him but didn't want to meet him. I think she shouldn't even have talked to him after she found out he was a stranger. Anyway, his calls were becoming more and more annoying and she was beginning to get nervous. She didn't know his name or what he looked like, and I too felt it was a little scary.

I told her, first, to check the corridor whenever she entered her room and not to open the door if a lone man was nearby. (I do this automatically all the time anyway. I just pretend to fumble for my key until he's walked past.) It helped that she was sharing the room with another woman. I suggested that whenever the other woman was there, she should be the one to answer the phone. If my friend was alone in the room when he called, I told her to hang up immediately. She'd already started doing that.

He must have got the idea because the calls ended. If she'd been occupying the room alone, stronger action might have been necessary. If it had been me, I'd have told the hotel manager about it and asked to have my room changed, and also made a fuss that they'd given out my name.

Dangerous Driving

Another type of scary situation is when a man decides to start a flirtation when you're both going 60 mph on the freeway. A woman alone in a car with out-of-state plates seems to attract these types, but it can happen right at home too. It usually starts when he passes you and does the neck-craning routine to get your attention. Then he pulls in right in front of you and slows down to 40 so you have to pass him. This dumb game continues until . . . actually, I have never been able to figure out what the turkey expects to happen next. Are you supposed to write your phone number in large letters with lipstick on the windshield? Roll down your window so he can toss a note in to you? Pull into the service area for a chat and a cup of coffee? Follow him into the rest area for a quickie on the grass?

It makes me angry because it's dangerous, passing and varying speed so much. The first thing to do when you notice the game is going on is to start concentrating very hard on your driving to avoid being in, or causing, an accident. If you can, fish for a pencil and write down his license plate number. Keep looking for the first chance to lose him. I watch for the next exit and make sure I'm behind him as we approach it, and then if he takes the exit I keep going, or if he doesn't exit, I do. I've never had the chance, but I've always wished I'd see a police patrol at the side of the road when this was happening. I'd just pull right in behind the cop with my flashers on and watch my "friend" keep going.

It can happen on city streets too. Two of my cousins were once being followed by a group of men in a car who kept shouting and waving their cans of beer to invite the girls to stop and get acquainted. My cousins were frightened because the men were obviously drunk and driving erratically. It was rush hour and there was heavy slow-moving traffic. What they decided to do has always delighted me. They drove out smack into the middle of a busy intersection and stopped, with the doors all locked and the windows rolled up. The ensuing chaos, with arm-waving, honking drivers all around them, attracted a cop within minutes. They told him they weren't going to move until the carload of men had left—which by this time, they very much wanted to do but couldn't because they were stuck in the traffic jam.

So many women have told me stories of being frightened when they noticed they were being followed by one or more men in another car that I went to talk to a private detective I know, an ex-cop. His advice was this: "A woman alone should always drive in her rearview mirror. Check often to see what cars are behind you, and if the same one seems to be there for too long, test to see if he's following you. You can do this by slowing down to see if he passes or whether he slows down too. If he stays behind you, get set for a right-hand turn, then make one as quickly as possible consistent with safety. Immediately after you turn, pull up to the curb and stop. If he turns right behind you, he'll have to keep going past you, and you can watch to see what he does. At this point he'll know that you know he's following you, if he is. Whatever you do, don't get out of your car. Most men will give up at this point. If he doesn't, you should be really worried. Keep driving until you see a policeman, or better yet, drive to the nearest police station and tell them what's going on."

If I wasn't paranoid before, that would do it.

All of the above should cover the ground pretty well on how to get rid of unwanted attentions. Let's go on to a more inspiring topic, what to do when exactly the reverse is true.

Meeting Strangers

I'll assume right from the start that you want to meet men, or else you wouldn't be reading this section. If you're married and still reading, that's up to you. My purpose is entirely practical, not moral.

As a matter of fact, how about that old double standard? United Airlines didn't include the question on its survey, so there's no way to tell how many married men are on the prowl when they're traveling, but I'd judge from my own very unscientific research that it's about 80 percent of them. If you're a married woman and want a little action on the side, a business trip is the ideal time for it. You keep it away from home and avoid all kinds of potential problems. As one man said to me recently, "I keep my street business on the street." That's kind of crude, but it says it all.

If your main objective is to get laid, married or single, by far the easiest way to do it is on a business trip. There are all those men out there, and nary a one with a wife or girlfriend along. You don't even need to do anything to meet them—just sit there. The best place to sit is in the bar of the hotel. Look around and take your pick.

But if you insist on being a little more choosy than that, there are certain difficulties. The greatest and most obvious of these is married men. According to United again, 84 percent of all traveling businessmen are married. It's significant that only 63 percent of traveling businesswomen are married. Married women more often choose not to travel, or don't get offered the jobs that require travel. They have to be at home to take care of the children and/or a husband. Why can't the husband do his share by taking care of the children while his wife travels? I'll consider it a big step toward liberation the day those percentages become the same.

There is something to be said in favor of an affair with a married man. Not much, but something. You know he's going to be discreet. If you too are married, that's a big plus. You may be less likely to get a disease from him. I'm trying to think of something else. Oh, yes—you'll have all that free time on weekends, Thanksgiving, Christmas. . . .

I met a very attractive man in Cleveland a few months ago. I was in the hotel cocktail lounge with three of my colleagues, and he was alone. He was so good-looking that I started to flirt with him, keeping it as cool as I could in front of the others. When I got up to go to the women's room, he followed me out. He introduced himself, and we talked for a moment in the corridor and made a date for dinner the next night.

Over dinner, I found out some things about him. He was a good conversationalist and we had many interests in common. He traveled often to the same cities I did. He was a very senior executive with my company's largest competitor. He was also very married and very interested in an affair. Without being the least bit crude or offensive, he spelled it out. He didn't make casual pick-ups and wasn't interested in waitresses or bar maids. He wanted a long-term relationship, not a one-night stand. He wanted to keep all the action outside of his home city. I was an ideal candidate. I told him no, and I never saw him again.

I've regretted it ever since. I shouldn't have said no, I should have said *maybe*. He would have been an extremely useful business acquaintance, after he found someone else who met his requirements for a mistress. I've always wished I'd done something to keep the relationship going a little while, to find out if it was possible to develop a platonic friendship with him.

If you want to find out if he's married, the most direct approach is to ask him. It's surprising how many men tell you the truth and say yes, and five minutes later you're admiring snapshots of his detestable little family. A lot of men lie too, especially those looking for a quick score. Then you need some more subtle ways of finding out. The wedding band, or the white place on his finger where it was a half-hour ago, is the standard giveaway, but very few men who are prepared to lie will make that mistake. A better test is whether he'll give you his home telephone number. If he's asked for yours and gotten it, and then you ask for his and he starts mumbling that he's hardly ever there and it's better to reach him at the office, forget it. On the other hand, some fancy steppers will give you a number that turns out to be the office number, or just plain phoney. If all he wants is a one-night stand, tonight, he has nothing to lose.

Judi Miller, author of *How to Ask a Man* (New York: Dell, 1978), has lots of good suggestions for finding out the truth. The best time to find out, of course, is before you even meet him. For example, she says, suppose you spot someone attractive in the supermarket. "Peanut butter and chopped meat means a single man. All the ingredients for a gourmet dinner can also be a single man. Pampers is not."

She has a whole chapter on married men, including case histories of women who not only got his home number and called him there, but went to his apartment, and even lived with him for months, before finding out he was married. She gives this advice:

1. Do you have his home phone number? Why not?
2. Have you ever been invited to his home? Why not?
3. If he tells you he is divorced, but you still suspect he is not, ask to see the divorce papers.

> If you're still not certain all this suspicion is necessary, or even healthy, remember, the danger in this potentially explosive situation is that, as time goes on, you may get more involved. And even if you're willing to date a married man, you won't be happy to wake up one day and realize you're in love with an accomplished liar.

Miller's book is more intelligent and better written than the title or cover blurb suggest. It's recommended reading for any woman who wants to learn some methods of improving her social life and her sex life.

Very often, being in a semi-business setting gives you an advantage. You may know, or get to meet, others who work with him. Knowing this, he may be less likely to lie to you. You can use the situation to check him out. When you get a chance to chat with one of his colleagues, you can say, "John seems like a very nice person. Does he have any children?" Or whatever you can work in without being too obvious. If you meet one of his female colleagues and can talk to her quietly for a few minutes, the question can be more direct—she's your ally and might want to know exactly the same thing about someone from your company.

(I'll know that the revolution has truly happened the day a book for men is published with a long discussion of how to find out if *she's* married.)

Returning to the 16 percent of the men on business trips who aren't married (assuming they didn't lie for the survey too), that's a discouraging figure. It's even more discouraging if you mentally eliminate those who are gay, too young, too old, under four feet tall, over 400 pounds, or otherwise unsuitable. After that, subtract the ones who are technically not married but living with someone, which is often just as good as being married.

Let's be optimistic and assume we've cut the potential pool of suitable, unmarried men by only half. That means that out of every hundred men you meet, eight will be worth finding out more about. And I haven't suggested you're looking for a husband or even a soulmate, now; just someone you might want to see again, spend a weekend with, or at the most optimistic, have a pleasant affair with. (Eight out of a hundred makes you want to reconsider the married ones. Remember the divorce rate.)

There is another consideration I haven't brought up yet, but maybe you've thought of it. What if you do meet a really interesting man and want to see him again, but he lives in San Diego and you live in Pittsburgh? *That's* enough to make you start reconsidering the one-night stand.

It happened to me just recently. We met at a three-day business conference in Atlanta. He was very attractive, divorced (I checked that out through business colleagues of his who were also attending), and was attracted to me. At coffee breaks and then over dinner we flirted and got better acquainted. He didn't make a pass at me, but I think if I'd wanted him to end up spending the last night in my room, that's the way it would have happened. Then the conference ended and he went back to Fort Lauderdale and I headed for Chicago. I still don't know if anything further is going to happen. We could easily arrange to be in the same city at the same time again. I've thought it over and decided to do nothing for the moment but wait and see if he's interested enough to get in touch with me.

In fact, I carried on an affair just like that for three years. I was based in Boston and he was on the West Coast. When you both travel often and look for ways and means, it's amazing how often you can get together.

Many of our meetings were "legitimate." For example, he went for his army reserve training near a city where there was a conference I honestly needed to attend; or he was flying from Seattle to New York with a flight connection in Chicago; or I was visiting a plant in Illinois and we met for three days in Chicago. We alternated taking our vacations on each other's side of the country. Some of our rendezvous were not so honest. He was being head-hunted by a firm back east, and went for an expense-paid interview even though he had no intention of considering the job. The headhunters unknowingly paid for a lovely weekend for the two of us.

In all, we saw each other eight or ten times a year, and were together anywhere from one day to a month. It ended when he met someone else and married her. I'll always wonder a little if it might have been different if I'd quit my job and found one closer to him. I couldn't bring myself to forfeit my independence to that extent; after all, if he was that interested he could have quit his job and. . . . I don't know. I do know I have some memories I wouldn't trade for anything. It was always play time because we never had the hassles of keeping house or trying to work out a budget.

If you can handle affairs like this, they can be tremendously exciting. You know each well enough to be very comfortable together, but after being apart for a month or two, the sexual tension when you meet again is almost unbearably good. It never gets routine or boring. You both have expense accounts, so it's nothing but the best restaurants and hotels. There's a new city to explore together, and no beds to make or garbage to be taken out. You have no other obligations, and from Friday to Sunday night, at the very least, you can party and make love. You see each other only when you're at your best; you can temporarily forget any problems waiting back home.

If this kind of lifestyle appeals to you, the way to meet the men to run it with is on your business trips. The trick is to meet as many as possible, to increase the odds of finding those eight in a hundred, or whatever the real figure may be. To accomplish that, you can't just sit in the bar. A less passive approach is called for. Spot the ones that look interesting and do something to make a meeting happen.

In other words, pick up men. If you've never done it and cringe at the idea, try Judi Miller's book for ideas and moral support and encouragement.

Old-fashioned travel books, that is, circa 1965, always tell you that the best way to meet men is to pretend that you're helpless. "For example," suggests one, "you buy a large street map, unfold it while standing at a busy intersection, and look puzzled. If ten minutes later you're still puzzled, head for another corner and try again." "If you want to make a man your friend," says another, "you should let him do you a favor. Being helpless, or pretending to be, is really an asset." Other recommendations include pretending you don't know how to work the air vent on the plane, or taking an extra-large piece of luggage that you have to struggle with.

Phooey.

In the first place, you're going to feel awfully silly if

the ploy works and in the course of the ensuing conversation you reveal that you've been flying to Chicago twice a week for the last three months because your project leader out there is in trouble, or that you run your own travel business. In the second place, it's deceitful. In the third place, the type of men you are likely to attract that way are those whose life philosophy is to keep females pregnant in the summer and barefoot in the winter. And finally, you will be betraying an enormous amount of work that other women have done to make it possible for you to be (rightfully) on that plane or street corner or wherever.

My theory is that if a man is offended or not interested in me because I make an approach to him, he's not my type anyway. I like very assertive men, those whose egos are strong enough to like it when a woman indicates she's interested and who are liberated enough not to be threatened by it.

One way is to walk up to a man and introduce yourself. I've done this a number of times, always in airports. I'm not sure why airports. Partly, I think, because they're so public I feel very safe. Also, just the fact that I'm there means that I'm on my way somewhere, or back, and meeting him is just incidental. And the fact that he's there, in a business suit and carrying an attaché case, tells you that at the very minimum he's likely to be employed, or if not, that he can afford to buy a plane ticket. Of course, he might be an escaped rapist on the run or a terrorist casing the place for a hijacking, but the odds are against it.

I was meeting a business colleague at San Francisco

airport. Getting off the plane right behind him was a very interesting-looking man, alone. Business suit and tie, check. Attaché case, check. No wedding ring, check. That all took about thirty seconds, and I had several minutes' more observation time as I chatted with my friend and we walked toward the baggage claim area. My prospect was headed in the same direction.

The bags started to come out on the conveyer, and I told my friend I'd avoid the crowd and step back. In the meantime, the man I was interested in had sat at a telephone kiosk, the type with no door, and he was thumbing through what looked like an address book, but he was not making any calls. This was getting better and better—no one to meet him and he's deciding whom to call.

I walked right over and said, "Hello, are you from San Francisco?" To my surprise he said, "Yes." No one to meet him in his home city? That must mean no wife. "Well," I said, fumbling for it because I had nothing prepared to say, "I've been here on business for two weeks, and you're the best thing I've seen." At first he was confused, then pleased, and he leaned back and started to smile. We were communicating. I told him I was with a business friend and had to drive him to the office, and offered my card with my local number. He dug out his business card and we swapped. He called me that afternoon, and we went out several times while I was there. Next time I go back, I'll look him up again. He was a nice person and we had fun together. If I hadn't been so bold, we never would have met.

It had taken me several years of thinking about it before I could get up the courage to make such a direct approach, and then I had to push myself to do it without thinking; if I'd hesitated any longer, I'd have lost my nerve. One thing that helps is to consider the absolute *worst* that could happen. He looks you up and down and says, "I wouldn't be seen dead with you if you paid me." Could you handle it? From a total stranger? Why, if he's that rude, and blind to boot, you're damned lucky to find out after having invested only a minute or two of your time. There's no rejection or put-down that can really hurt you. You have nothing to lose.

One item was a tremendous aid in the San Francisco incident, and has been many times before and since. That is The Business Card. *Love* that business card. It establishes instantly that you have some status, it tells him something about you from your job title and what company you work for, and it gives him your name and office phone number. No fumbling for a pencil and the awkwardness of spelling names. It puts the information he needs right in his hand, in a very polite way, but without any obligation. If he wants to he can toss the card in the nearest waste basket. Most men are so intrigued they don't, of course. And it has an important further advantage—every man automatically reaches for *his* business card to give to you. Swapping and collecting business cards is so widely done it's almost a reflex action. Now you know something about him, including where he's employed. Everything's on an equal footing, and in a couple of seconds you've both established that you're probably legitimate people.

I don't even go to the laundromat without my business card case. It's useful in any situation where you might meet someone you'd like to get to know better, whether it's on a plane, in a hotel bar, anywhere.

If you don't have business cards, get some. If your company refuses to issue them, get them printed yourself. Any job shop printer will do a large batch for about $25. Take along something with the company name and logo on it so they can copy it onto the card. This is perfectly honest and legal, provided you really do work there. The only thing about it to give pause is that it's so easy; anyone who wanted to could have an assortment of business cards, all phoney. Of all the hundreds I've collected, though—many of them in straightforward business meetings—not one has turned out to be bogus, to my knowledge.

Gay Women

I wanted to include a section here for gay women on questions of whether, or how far, to come out of the closet and how to meet others. I've met several women in recent years who I liked very much and who revealed, quite early in our friendship, that they were gay. I felt a little awkward trying to include such a section in the book because I'm interested only in men and have never made the gay scene.

I asked the women I knew, and some gay men too, and was told not to worry about it. There are support groups, organizations, and clubs for gays that form an underground network. If you're gay and happy about it, you'll know where to make contacts and how to find where the gay scene is. It exists in every big city, San Francisco and Atlanta being the two cities with the largest gay populations in the United States. There are always gay bars for men, and some where women are welcome. In a few places there are gay bars and discos that cater exclusively to women.

Since that's all I know about the subject, I'll stop.

One-Night Stands

The question of whether or not to indulge in one-night stands becomes even more perplexing when you travel a lot. For one thing, there are so many opportunities, and for another, there's that problem of what to do if the two of you live far apart.

As a rule, I don't, at least not intentionally. The reason is pragmatic rather than moral: for me, sex is always better the second, and third, and fourth time, and so on. It's partly because I'm nervous the first time, and partly because, as with many women, a large part of my sexual enjoyment is in my head. If it was good the first time, I think how much better it's going to be as we get to know each other's preferences, and looking forward to it enhances the pleasure.

The closest I've come to it, knowing in advance it was never going to happen again, was for a one-weekend-stand. We had met briefly a few weeks before at a business lunch. He called me at the office on Friday afternoon and said, "I've just gotten a big promotion and a transfer to Germany. I broke up with a woman I was seeing steadily a few months ago and I have nobody to celebrate with. Will you go to Miami with me for the weekend?" I thought about it for about four seconds and said, "Yes." I figured that at the very worst, I'd do some work toward keeping my tan from fading.

As it turned out, we could have saved some money and stayed at home. Once we got to the hotel room we didn't leave it for the entire weekend. All meals—when we remembered to eat—were from room service. For me, some of the initial excitement was from being with him at the airport and in the plane, knowing I was going to go to bed with this very attractive stranger. For both of us, part of it was knowing we had only the weekend. He was leaving for his new job the next week, and it was before the days of supersonic planes—even so, carrying on an affair between different continents would have been impossible.

As I got to know him a little I knew that we would never be a regular couple anyway. His politics would have infuriated me, and I liked all the sports he hated and vice versa. So there were no regrets when we parted, and I have some memories that, ten years later, have become such good sexual fantasies that I'm no longer sure what really happened and what I've invented. It was perfect just as it was.

So I can understand women who extol the virtues of

the one-night stand. There is that little edge of excitement that will never be there again. If you have no intention of seeing him again, you're less likely to do things just to please him and make him like you, and more apt to concentrate on your own pleasure. And if it's a flop, so what? On to the next one.

You can think it over and decide for yourself.

10

Conventions, Conferences, and Seminars

The statistics show that for many women, their first experience of business travel is to attend a conference or convention of some kind. These events are part of the American Way of Business. More and more women are getting, or creating, the opportunity to go on training courses and seminars too.

In some respects these occasions are different from a sales trip or going to one of your company's other sites for a meeting or consultation activity. You might be your company's only representative, which may imply some kind of special responsibility for presenting the right "image" to outsiders, and also means that everyone you meet will be a stranger to you. On the other hand, you are there as part of a more or less large audience, which gives you a certain degree of anonymity. At least it does in theory; being one of thirty women at a convention of five hundred men ensures that you *can't* fade into the background, however much you might like to.

If you're a speaker at the conference, that presents a special set of problems by itself. I remember the time I was one of several guest speakers at a computer managers' conference. The audience and the other speakers were all men. I was wearing a new blouse, one I hadn't worn before. Wearing new clothes for an occasion like that is never to be recommended, and I should have known better. I was given one of those small portable microphones that a man clips to his necktie. I had to clip it to the lapel of my blouse. The buttonholes on that blouse were just a little bit too large for their buttons. The weight of the microphone dragging at the fabric kept unbuttoning the blouse. I spent most of the time buttoning it back up again. I doubt very much whether anyone actually heard anything that I said, but on the rating forms handed in by the audience at the end of the day, I had top scores for "presentation style" and "usefulness of information."

Public speaking is a topic that requires a book of its own, though, so I'm going to assume for the rest of this chapter that you're a member of the audience.

Men

Just about everything I said in the chapter on men goes double at conferences and conventions. Somehow, the setting combined with the male-bonding syndrome turns some ordinary guys into drooling sex maniacs.

A young woman on our staff attended her first conference recently and came back quite shaken by the experience. She said she just wasn't prepared for the kinds of remarks that men made to her. "Honey, it's so nice to have you to look at when the speaker gets boring" and, "What's a pretty little thing like you doing here?" are some of the milder comments she got. She felt so nonplussed and even a little threatened by some of these approaches that she started skipping the cocktail parties and other after-hours gatherings.

There's no way to prevent these incidents, no matter how businesslike you are in appearance and behavior. You'll head off some of them by acting all business, but a few are inevitable. The best thing to do is to ignore them or treat them as a joke, depending on the remark and the circumstances.

Unfortunately, the tone for this type of male behavior is often set by the conference speakers. Every speaker feels compelled to start off with a few jokes, and many of the jokes are sexist. I think that if I hear the line, "Bringing your wife to a conference is like going hunting with a gamekeeper" once more, I'm going to throw up.

Don't stay away from the social gatherings and dinners because of it, though. There is an "old-boy network" in the business world that is largely developed and supported by these occasions. It's an opportunity to cultivate business relationships with people who could be useful to you—and you to them—throughout your career. Contacts are made, jobs sought and candidates recruited, sales opportunities opened, business cross-talk and introductions exchanged—all very useful. That's why such semisocial events are held, and they are sometimes the unofficial but primary reason for the conference or convention in the first place.

After the third or fourth round of drinks, however, you may decide to excuse yourself and just not return. The business value of the occasion dwindles to nil about the time someone offers to give you his room key or suggests that the two of you go somewhere else "to get better acquainted."

On the other hand, there was one memorable incident at a seminar my company was sponsoring, with attendees from many different organizations. Half-way through the week the hotel manager approached me and my colleague, as we were the official organizers and sponsors of the event, to tell us that two of the men attending had moved into the same room together. We figured that was their business and told the hotel manager just to ignore it.

Considering the possibility that you might meet a man you'd like to know better for non-business reasons, however, a seminar or conference is one of the best places for it. You can spend time in each other's company in public, to get to know each other, without making any implied commitment. You can see him several times during the course of the event, and so don't have to make a snap decision about whether to accept a date or invite him to your room until you're ready to. The setting gives these preliminaries an air of legitimacy, and neatly solves the problem of whether to pick up men by making it unnecessary.

Incidentally, it's always understood at these events that by virtue of the fact that you're both attendees, no formal introduction is required. It's totally acceptable to say to the stranger standing nearby, "What company are you with?" (if you're not wearing badges) or, "What did you think of the speaker?" If the conversation develops a little further, that's the time to get out your business card to give to him. And ask for his, if it isn't immediately offered.

Dress

Unless the conference brochure or other literature you get before attending says otherwise, take your everyday business clothes. Sometimes, a seminar will be held at a resort area or in an informal setting where the dress code is relaxed. In that case, the organizers will say so in the advertisements or when your registration is made. If you're not sure, call and ask them ahead of time.

As I indicated in the chapter on packing, your business clothes are always appropriate for evening events too. The rule of thumb is, if it's an occasion to which the men will be wearing business suits, you can do the same. A more dressy outfit is not necessary. If in doubt, you can take along a cocktail dress or an evening skirt with the appropriate accessories, and then decide from the tone of the proceedings whether to leave it in the closet or not. If there are other women, you might consult with them to see what they're planning to wear to the dinner or dinner/dance.

Outside Activities

Don't feel that you're trapped by the event or are required to spend all your time at organized activities. You don't have to spend all afternoon listening to a boring speaker who isn't telling you anything you didn't know, or hold up the bar until it closes.

If the event is really a flop, of course, totally useless as a business event, you should leave right away and have your company ask for the fee back. Write a letter or a memo explaining why. But if you just want to use the lunch hour to do some shopping or an evening to explore the city or look up old friends, do so. I don't have any figures on how many people actually attend all the sessions of a conference, but it's quite low, I'm sure. At one conference my company gave recently, as we discovered later, a handful of the attendees spent most of their time at a twenty-four-hour poker game going on in one of the hotel rooms.

11

Overseas

A business trip to a foreign country is always highly prized. It's somehow much more special to go to Paris, France, than to Paris, Texas. Even if you've had vacations overseas, a business trip is different. First of all, of course, all your expenses are paid. But also, you'll see the country from an entirely different angle, and have a much better chance to learn how the natives really live. You meet different kinds of people, not just those whose livelihood is serving tourists; and their attitude toward you is different. In fact, I'd much rather see a foreign country as a business traveler, even if only a small part of my time is spent on business, than as a vacationer.

In this chapter, I'm not going to give a country-by-country analysis of places to meet men or sights to see. I am going to talk about principal ways in which overseas business travel differs from travel in America, and give you the benefit of my experience on how to get the most out of the trip, both as a business activity and as an opportunity to learn about how the rest of the world lives.

Preparation

In spite of my comment in an earlier chapter, three days in London is somewhat different from three days in Kansas City, if only by virtue of the fact that you have to do a little more advance planning. At the minimum, you'll need a passport, and for some countries you'll need a visa and certain health documents. Check this out through your travel agent or the local consulate of the country you're visiting. Do it as far in advance as possible. Requirements for immunizations vary from time to time, and many people have adverse reactions to some of the shots. I once had to get smallpox and yellow fever immunizations at the same time and was sick in bed for three days. (Luckily, smallpox occurs rarely now, thanks to the World Health Organization.) Sometimes you need the immunization not to get into the country you're visiting but to get back into the U.S. afterward. Don't leave it until the last minute to find out.

Also find out about U.S. Customs rules; these change from time to time and can influence what you buy overseas. If you're taking an expensive item, such as a camera, that was manufactured overseas but purchased here, be sure you can prove where you bought it or you might end up having to pay duty again. Take the sales slip or register the item with U.S. Customs before you leave.

When you're packing, remember that your belongings are going to be pawed over not only by airline security staff but by customs inspectors at each stop too. And a further point here: check with the airline about luggage restrictions. Within the U.S., weight is no longer a consideration, but it still is for most overseas travel. If you're buying heavy items to bring back, it's often cheaper to have them shipped than to pay for overweight luggage. A further advantage to sending things home is that gifts that are sent rather than carried with you are considered separately for import duty, not counted toward your total.

One of the most important steps you can take in preparation is to visit a bookstore or library for some guidebooks about the country or city you'll be visiting. Check in the front of the book to see when it was published—this type of information gets out of date rapidly. I recommend more than one source because every author has his or her own preferences. If you find the same recommended sight or warning in two or more books, it's probably worth considering. Use these not just for lists of places to see, but also for information about local practices and customs. It's very useful to know, for example, that you can't get dinner in Paris before about 7 P.M., because the restaurants don't open until then, or that it's just the opposite in Ireland: if you wait until after 8 P.M., everything's closed and you'll starve. Or that in England, "tea" means a snack and "high tea" means a hearty meal; or that in Madrid, if your hosts say they'll meet you at 10 P.M. to go out, that means *dinner*, which will last until midnight.

Another good investment is a small phrase book, if you don't speak the language. Most educated foreigners speak English quite well (a condemnation of our own educational system, which turns out very few students equipped to speak any foreign language well), and unless instructed otherwise, it's safe to assume that those you'll be doing business with can speak English. (At conferences and the like, there are usually simultaneous-translation facilities.) But knowing a few phrases in the language is courteous and can be useful to help you identify the women's room, nonsmoking areas, first-class train compartments, taxi stands, drugstores, and other basic survival necessities. Pay special attention to the menu section. I would estimate that for any language that uses the Roman alphabet, two or three hours of study and private practice should give you enough words to be able to order something you can identify on the menu and to be able to say "please," "thank you," and other basic courtesy phrases.

Communicating your desires and understanding what other people are saying are not the same things, however. You find this out the first time you walk up to a stranger, having carefully rehearsed your question, to ask how to get to the Street of the Seven Knives, and then listen to a five-minute discourse, with gesticulations, not a word of which you understand.

Which leads to the next piece of advice: get a map of the area and study it. If you can't pronounce the name of the street, you can just point to it. Mark the location of your hotel, the airport, the office, and other places you'll be going, in order to orient yourself. It's embarrassing to leap into a taxicab and ask for a destination that turns out to be halfway down the block.

One type of arrangement *not* to make in advance is for excursions by air that you'll be paying for yourself. At the peak of the local vacation season, you might have to—but avoid it if you can. The reason for this is that if you make reservations locally you can often get cheaper rates. If you're in London, for example, and want to go to just about any other European city for the weekend, you can get air fare or a package deal (air fare plus hotel) much cheaper. You have to be there to do it, it can't be arranged through your American travel agent. Go to a travel agent in your base city, or to the local American Express office.

Currency

Get at least a small amount of money in the currencies of the countries you'll be visiting, in advance. (Order it at your bank.) Make sure it includes some coins, preferably at least one of every type. This is tip and taxi money, and also helps you to familiarize yourself with it. There's no excuse for treating all foreign currency like funny-money, and it's discourteous to the citizens of the place you're visiting. (Anyway, it's U.S. dollars that are funny-money in many places these days.) I've seen tourists helplessly hold out a handful of change, or always pay with a large bill because they couldn't count it out themselves. Besides being discourteous, this sets you out as an easy person to cheat, and you *will* be cheated, sooner or later, in spite of what you may have heard about the honesty of foreigners in not taking advantage of "trusting" Americans.

You'll probably also want to take traveler's checks. I take as little money as possible this way because I don't like giving a double profit to the companies that put them out. You pay once for the checks, and then they have the use of your money until you cash them. One ad even encourages you not to cash in what you have left over after the trip. This is called "the float"—checks issued that haven't been used. It's an interest-free loan to the traveler's-check company.

As a business traveler, you may have an advantage in having check-cashing and currency exchange privileges through the local office of your company. You'll probably get the best exchange rate there, equal to the bank rate, without having to pay any charge. Next best is a bank. Hotels and shops give you the worst exchange rates.

Attitudes

One of the most important items you can take with you is the right attitude. That means being prepared for the fact that some things will be different, but also remembering that different does not mean worse. At the very least, you will annoy your host in Germany by asking if the water is safe to drink, and create a bad impression of all Americans by complaining when you don't find everything to be exactly the way it is at home.

With an open mind, you will probably find that in many countries, some things are *better* than at home. In England, I decided that putting the toilet and the bathtub in two different rooms was much more civilized and hygienic; in France, that it is possible to have an efficient postal system; in Italy, that Americans have a long way to go to learn how to cook seafood properly. Try not to carry along all your stereotypes too. You'll be disappointed if you don't get pinched black and blue in Italy, if a German doesn't click his heels, or a Frenchman doesn't kiss your hand.

Be prepared, though, for the stereotypes that foreigners have of Americans. I was once told, "But you can't be a Yank, you're too soft-spoken." Another time, I was on a bus in London when an elderly couple, obviously up from the country for a special occasion, asked me for directions. I whipped out my map of the city and showed them their street. They thanked me and then the woman turned to her husband and said, "You see? So efficient!"

If you're visiting a culture that has drastically different expectations for the behavior of women, it's even more important to study your guidebooks to find out what these differences are, and to ask the advice of other travelers and of local business people you'll be dealing with.

A pantsuit may be a major social problem, for example, embarrassing your hosts by making it impossible for them to take you to a local restaurant. On the other hand, as a Westerner and especially as an American, you can get away with things the native woman can't, such as going on the street without a veil. Americans aren't expected to know any better. Don't use this to deliberately upset people, but it can be useful when you've made a real goof in etiquette.

For example, I was once in a taxi with a British business colleague. When it came time to pay the fare, I said "I'll toss you for it." His chin dropped about three feet and he turned bright red. I later found out that "toss you" is English slang for "feel you up." I got away with it because I was a naive Yank.

It's also useful know such things as the fact that the English word "computer" is very close to the Spanish word meaning prostitute; and that to an Englishman, "fanny" is much closer in meaning to "cunt" than it is to "ass." But like me, you'll probably find out the hard way.

Culture Shock

Culture shock is the paralysis that hits you when you suddenly realize you're alone in a foreign country where you don't speak the language and aren't sure whether any of the most basic rules of behavior you have been taught since childhood will apply. In extreme forms, tourists have been known to almost starve to death from culture shock, because they were too terrified to leave the hotel room in search of something to eat. The less Western the country the more likely you are to suffer from it, but it can happen even in English-speaking countries.

Some of the advice I gave a little earlier, such as boning up with a guidebook and learning a few phrases in the language, will help. It also helps a lot if you are visiting a business site; there are people there who can give advice and help you find your way around, and who have probably dealt with culture-shocked Americans before. If you've visited the country before, that helps too. The best aid is having a traveling companion to share the troubles with and laugh with when *ananas* turns out to be pineapple, not bananas, or when you walk into a rest room and find it's coed. Or worse yet, that it's a hole in the ground. Or when you continually get off the elevator at the wrong floor because "One" is the second floor.

Culture shock is compounded by jet lag, which can be a serious problem by itself.

Jet Lag

Jet lag is the disorientation and malaise that results from experiencing a sudden change in time zones. It's more than just being faced with a heavy dinner when your stomach thinks it's breakfast time. Your sleep pattern is disrupted too, along with other diurnal body rhythms. For reasons that no one seems to understand fully, there are measurable effects on a person's ability to make rational judgments and decisions when jet-lagged. It is for this reason that many companies have a rule that executives may not sign contracts or make any business decisions for a certain number of days after crossing a specified number of time zones.

The first thing to do is to be aware that it's going to happen to you. It helps to know that the feeling you have that *anything* is too much trouble and that you're terrified to go out on the street is partly physiological, normal, and transitory. You will get over it, you're not coming down with polio or a nervous breakdown.

Allow yourself time to get acclimated before plunging into business. This means planning your travel to arrive at the start of a weekend, preferably on Friday, so you have several days to take it easy and get adjusted. Don't plan a lot of strenuous sightseeing for the first few days either.

The most valuable trick to know about, though, is to *immediately* start living by the new time. When you get on the plane, set your watch to the equivalent of the time at your destination and try to start thinking that way. For example, from the East Coast to most places in Europe, the time change is plus five hours. That is, if you take off at 5 P.M., it's already 10 P.M. at your destination, and when you land it'll be 5 A.M., even though your body tells you it's just midnight. *Don't go to sleep.* By the time you get to your hotel and get settled in, it'll be breakfast time locally. Have breakfast and stay awake for most of the day. An early bedtime is OK. But don't immediately go to sleep for eight or ten hours. You'll wake up rarin' to go just at dinnertime, and then not be able to sleep until the next dawn, and the pattern will continue until you show up at the office on Monday bleary-eyed and exhausted. The sooner you start keeping the local time, the easier it is to adjust and the sooner you'll get over the jet lag.

I know some travelers who cope by just staying on their home time. This works all right if you're only going to be there a few days, and if you can get breakfast at 9 P.M. and dinner at 5 A.M. And convince the local business people to accommodate you. But you can't change what time the sun rises and sets so there will be some disorientation anyway.

Going in the other direction, east-west, the problem still exists but it seems to be less severe for many people. Let's say, London to Los Angeles: you arrive at 10 P.M. local time, which would be 6 A.M. where you came from. You're tired from the trip, and you'll probably have no trouble getting to sleep, even though you slept on the plane; also, you'll wake up at a normal local hour.

Returning home is usually less trouble for most people too. For one thing, you're coming back to familiar surroundings and don't have the culture shock to contend with. For another, unless you've been away for a month or more, you never did get fully adjusted even if it seemed like it, so returning to your "natural" time is easier.

Health and Safety

Many of the suggestions I've given earlier in the book for health and safety apply equally to foreign travel. Many foreign countries are reputed to have lower crime rates than the U.S., and the streets are safer for women alone. It is said that you can drop a diamond ring in the center of the square in Brussels, and come back a year later to find a local resident keeping an eye on it for your return. Even so, it can't hurt to lock your hotel room door and take all the other precautions you would in America. I recommend that you do so.

Study your guidebooks and ask the travel agent and other travelers about any special health precautions you should take. In some parts of the world, this means not eating any raw fruits or vegetables or not drinking tap water. (But I've seen paranoid tourists, who even brushed their teeth in bottled water, sitting at the bar drinking drinks with ice cubes that were no doubt made from tap water.) Other places, it means not eating any rare meat, shaking out your shoes before putting them on, and not sitting down on the toilet seat until you've carefully checked that the bowl is not inhabited. Some special medications may be required—for example, if you're visiting a place where malaria is endemic. You may need to start taking the pills before you leave and continue for a while after you get back. Find out in advance about these things.

Keeping Clean

When you are anywhere outside of North America you should always have two things on your person: your passport and some cash. The cash first. In some countries it is a crime to be on the street or in a public place without a certain amount of cash. No matter what you have in traveler's checks or credit cards, no cash means a vagrant. Technically, you could be arrested if you're stopped by the police and don't have any cash. *In the local currency.* The equivalent of about $50 U.S. should be enough, if you haven't checked the local law.

It is also *a crime* in many places not to carry identification. A passport is excellent identification. There is a further advantage to always having your passport with you, which is that you are less likely to have it stolen. The dumbest thing you can do overseas is to lose your passport. First of all, you can't leave wherever you are without it, and even if you could, you can't get back into the United States without it. You can get a lost passport replaced at the nearest United States Embassy. (It's in the phone book under U for United States, or E for États-Unis, or whatever the local language is. Not, as some tourists have been known to think, under A for America.) It's a time-consuming and frustrating procedure though. If the passport was stolen, you'll probably have to go through another long rigmarole with the local police.

Carrying your passport with you all the time means *all* the time. Don't put it in your briefcase, because you're apt to go out to lunch or dinner without that. If it won't fit in your small evening bag, stick it down your panty hose or use a larger handbag. Don't rely on your companion to carry it, even if he's your husband. You could get separated in a crisis.

I once made a reverse exception to this rule by carrying someone else's passport. We were traveling around Europe together, and he was totally hopeless at keeping track of documents. Every time we got to a checkpoint or a ticket counter, he'd start madly searching through all his pockets and baggage for his documents, while the official in front of us frowned and the tourists behind us muttered. I finally got so tired of it that I appointed myself Keeper of the Documents, and we got around much faster that way. I gave him his back when we got where we were going though.

Don't take chances about the local laws in foreign countries. This means use some common sense—if in doubt, don't smoke it, don't carry it, don't sell it, don't buy it, and don't photograph it. Not all countries will give you the "rights" you expect at home. For example, France does not have the concept of *habeas corpus*. That means they can legally arrest you and keep you totally incommunicado indefinitely—no phone call, no lawyer, no trial. The U.S. Embassy will not leap to your rescue, especially if you have broken a law. After a week or so in jail, you might get a visit from a junior American diplomat who'll tell you there's nothing they can do for you.

If you're sharing a hotel room with a man you're not married to, check out the local laws and customs, or be careful and play it by ear. In England, for example, they don't care as long as you register as husband and wife. In France, they don't care as long as you use your real names. The English respect privacy and convention above all—they don't demand to see your identification, and would be embarrassed if you used different names. The French are concerned with the law, which requires you to hand over your passport (the police go around to all hotels to look at passports of new arrivals—you get it back in the morning), but they don't give a damn about morality.

Some of the suggestions I've made in this chapter may make it sound like foreign travel is rife with hazards and problems. If it is so, that's only because it's different, not because it's more dangerous. Someone from a tropical climate who is in the habit of inspecting the bedclothes before getting in to make sure there aren't any scorpions, and of boiling all water before drinking it, may find the dangers of walking in Central Park after dark and the sight of rats in the New York City subway much more terrifying. It all depends on what you're used to, which is also what makes foreign travel so interesting: it *is* different.

12

The Corporate Gypsy

There is a small band of travelers in America known as corporate gypsies. They are often salespersons but may be auditors, consultants, or others whose jobs require close to one-hundred-percent travel. For almost a year and a half I was a member of this tribe, so I can speak about it knowledgeably.

For some people, the gypsy life is a full-time commitment. For many others, as it was for me, the job comes with the understanding that it will end in a promotion or a transfer after a year or two.

Many people, given this choice, find it an excellent opportunity. It gives them a chance to see the country at the company's expense. In some organizations, it gives a wide exposure to the company's business and the opportunity to develop contacts that will be valuable career assets for years ahead. I know some people who use it as a way to "shop around" for a more permanent job in a community they like.

Furthermore, living full-time on an expense account can be extremely lucrative. If you're single with no dependents, there's no reason to maintain a house or apartment. You have very few living expenses that aren't company-paid, and you can use your per diem or expense account money to live on and put your paycheck in the bank. I've known people who used this chance to accumulate the downpayment on a house very rapidly, or to put away enough for a year or two of further travel on their own in Europe, or to build up a respectable investment portfolio.

No Fixed Abode

If you're traveling this way and can stand the idea, it could be smart to give up your apartment or rent out your house for the duration. Be careful, though, that the IRS doesn't classify you as an *official* corporate gypsy. That means that all your expense money is taxable income, which wipes out most of the financial advantage. Keep a legal residence somewhere. Sublet your apartment on a month-by-month basis, keeping your name on the lease; or move back to your parents' house and claim that as your legal residence. If you're not long out of college, you might do that anyway. Or move your furniture to a relative's house and pay rent, which is what I did. Double-check this with your company's tax department or a tax accountant to be sure that your expenses are not going to be classed as taxable income.

Problems

This type of lifestyle is not for everyone, of course, even on a short-term basis. I've known some people—as many men as women—who tried it and couldn't stand being away from home all the time (excepting possibly Christmas and vacations—imagine going home for your vacation as a special treat!).

This lifestyle can be very lonely; corporate gypsies find it extremely difficult to maintain long-term relationships. Few married people try it, and those that do tend not to remain married very long. Among younger people, engagements are made and broken with startling rapidity. If you're *both* on the move a lot, you may see more of each other than if one isn't—I discussed this possibility in the chapter on men.

There is the further problem of stress. No matter how independent you are, you need personal relationships and someone to talk to. Spending all your time alone or with strangers is not conducive to the best mental health, nor is the continual danger, however slight, of always being on the road and staying in hotels.

This problem is alleviated somewhat if you have friends and relatives around the country to visit and even to stay with. (It's difficult to turn new acquaintances into friends when you're moving on in a few weeks.)

I would recommend, too, that if you're going to be in one spot for more than a few weeks you try to find an apartment or house to sublet or share. This was the tactic I employed, and it worked quite well. In some cities, friends scouted the possibilities for me and found, for example, someone whose roommate had just moved out and who needed a paying guest, short-term, to help with the rent.

In other places I used the classified ads for houses to share. Even if the person is looking for a permanent roommate, if you offer twice as much rent as they're asking, you can often make a deal. Be wary, though, of men who use these ads to find a sex partner. A clue is when you call about the apartment and they ask what you look like. On the other hand, I've shared places with male roommates on several occasions, without hassles. Just be sure he knows that it's strictly a business arrangement, and you intend to keep your bedroom door locked. If you have any doubts at all, pass it up.

At other times, I've found short-term furnished apartment rentals that were very nice. This is easiest in cities with large tourist trades. Even if you're paying what seems an exorbitant rent, it's still cheaper than a hotel at $30 or $40 a night—that's $900 or more a month, and for that money you can find a super pied-à-terre, even paying a premium for very short-term use. You're more comfortable, and the company likes it because it's saving money. Everybody wins.

There are practical difficulties too. For example, what do you do about getting needed work done on your teeth? In many cities you can't even get a dentist appointment in less than six weeks, and by that time you'll be gone. The only solution here is to plan ahead—make advance appointments with your home dentist for when you know you'll be there, insisting on a visit every day for a week if necessary; or, call ahead and get a recommendation for your next port-of-call. It may be difficult explaining why you don't have a home address in that city, but with a little imagination you'll manage.

Credit companies look at you askance—a permanent residence is one of the prime requirements for a bank loan or credit card. It doesn't matter how good your salary is, they just don't understand. Or, how do you cash a check out-of-state (ever tried it?) when *everywhere* is out-of-state? (The solution to this is to use the local company's petty-cash fund for check-cashing.)

If you like the lifestyle and you like your work, these difficulties can be overcome, though. And once you're accustomed to the gypsy life, staying in one place can get very tedious. I've seen gypsies who, after two weeks in one city, start making desperate arrangements to get away somewhere *different* for a weekend.

Even when you're ready to give it up and succumb to the nesting instinct by settling in one place, there's always a certain amount of nostalgia left. You think about the Manhattan skyline at night, the fog rolling in under the Golden Gate Bridge, those glorious glimpses of Mount Rainier, the dark pines and white churches of New England, the almost sexual *thrum* of the plane engines at takeoff, dancing all night in an Atlanta disco, dusk on a rainy road into Indianapolis, and all the truckers' CB chatter as the white line unrolls for miles and miles past your car . . . could you ever really stay home again?

Index

Adult bookstores, 129
Affairs, *see* Men; Sexual relationships
Air conditioning for cars, 45
Air express, 18
Airports: inspection of luggage at, 34–35; meeting men in, 161–62
Air travel, 65–83; with babies and children, 74, 82–83; bumping, 70–71; carry-on luggage for, 23–27, 34–36; clothes to wear for, 37–39; comfort in, 79–82; connecting flights, 66, 67; delays, 71; double-booking, 70; fares, 67–68; fear of, 77; food, 102–3; insurance, 78–79; Official Airline Guide, 66–67, 69; personal or business emergencies, 82; safety tips, 76–79; seating arrangements, 72–75, 80; stand-by and wait-list options, 68–70; time-saving techniques, 75–76; *See also* Overseas travel
Apartments to share or sublet, 194–95
Appliances, 25–26
Attitudes, 6–14
Auto mechanics, course on, 53
Automobile travel, 37, 41–63; books on, 63; car maintenance, 52–55; choice of car, 42–44; driving skills, 48–52; freeway driving, 56–61; options and accessories for car, 44–48; packing for, 27–29; safety tips, 60–63; sexual advances from men in other cars, 150–53

Bars, 124–26; gay, 165
Boots, 25
Bottles, plastic, 25
Braking, left-foot, 51–52

197

INDEX

Briefcase, 24
Burger King, 105, 107
Business cards, 163–64

California, car inspection entering, 34
Calisthenics, 134, 135
Car travel, see Automobile travel
Carry-on bags, 23–27, 34–36
CB radios, 46–48
Clothes, 18, 19; for conferences and conventions, 173–74; evenings, 31; packing, 30, 32; traveling, 37–39
Conferences and conventions, 169–74
Corporate gypsies, 191–96
Cosmetics, 32, 34
Culture shock, 182–83
Currency, foreign, 179–80
Customs, U.S., 176–77

Delays, air travel, 71
Dental problems, 141, 195
Depression, 137, 138
Diet, 93–97; See also Eating
Discos, 124, 125
Dress, see Clothes
Driving, see Automobile travel
Driving skills, 48–52
Drunk men, sexual advances from, 147–48, 152–53

Ear popping, on airplanes, 80–81
Eating, 93–111; do it yourself, 100–2; in fast-food restaurants, 104–9; freeway, 103–9; fruits and vegetables, 98–100, 105, 106, 108; gourmet, 109–11; on planes, 102–3; in restaurants, 93–99
Emergencies, health, 140–42
European airports, security checks in, 35
Evening outfits, 31
Exchange rates, 180
Exercise, 133–38
Eyes, air travel and, 80

Fast-food restaurants, 104–9
Flirtation, 145, 150–51
Food, see Eating
Foreign countries, see Overseas travel
Freeway: driving on, 56–61; eating on the, 103–9
French fries, 106
Fruits, 98–100, 105, 106, 108

Garment bag, 23–25
Gay women, 164–65
Geography, 117–19
Guidebooks, 177–78

Handbag, 24–25
Health, overseas travel and, 185–86
Health clubs, 135–37
Holiday rush periods, air travel during, 69
Hospital emergency rooms, 141
Hotels (or motels), 85–92; choosing, 85–86; locking up your valuables, 90; reservations, 86–88; safety tips, 88–90; services offered by, 90–91

Houses to share or sublet, 194–95

Immunizations for overseas travel, 176
Income tax, corporate gypsies and, 192–93
Insurance, air travel, 78–79
Ironing clothes, 26

Jazz clubs, 124
Jet lag, 183–85
Jogging, 134

Kentucky Fried Chicken, 106, 107

Lists of things to pack, 30, 32
Lodging: alternatives to hotels or motels, 91–92; *See also* Hotels
Log, car maintenance, 55
Lonesomeness, 137, 139
Luggage, 17–36, 75; airport inspection of, 34–35; carry-on, 23–27, 34–36; hints for packing, 33–34; locking, 36; name tags on, 22; roller attachment or wheels for, 20; shopping for, 22–23; soft-sided versus hard-sided, 20–22

McDonald's, 105–7
Men, 143–67; in bars, 125–26; at conferences and conventions, 171–73; meeting, 153–64; picking up, 160–64; turning down advances from strangers, 148–53; *See also* Sexual relationships
Menstruation, 139–40
Mental health, 137–39, 193
Miller, Judi, 156–57, 160
Molloy, John T., 21, 31–32, 43
Motels, *see* Hotels
Movie theaters, going alone to, 119, 122
Music: automobile travel and, 28, 46; concerts and recitals, 123

Newspapers, underground or alternative, 114–15
Nightclubs, 124–26

Official Airline Guide, 66–67, 69
Oil change, automobile, 54
One-night stands, 165–67
Overseas travel, 175–89; attitudes and, 180–82; carrying your passport and cash, 186–88; culture shock and, 182–83; currency and, 179–80; health and safety tips for, 185–86; jet lag, 183–85; laws and customs and, 188–89; preparation for, 176–79

Packing, 17–36; for overseas travel, 177; planning, 29–33; *See also* Luggage
Passport, 186, 187
Penknife, 100–1
Phrase books, 178
Plastic bottles, 25
Potatoes, 97, 106

INDEX

Radios: car, 46; CB, 46–48, 62
Reading, 126–28
Restaurants, 92–99, 115; fast-food, 104–9; going alone to, 119–22; gourmet, 110–11; reading in, 127; tips in, 121, 122
Rivers, 118

Safety tips: for automobile travel, 60–63; for air travel, 76–79; for hotels and motels, 88–90; for overseas travel, 185–86
Salads, 95, 96
Seat belts; airplane, 77–78; automobile, 45–46
Sexual relationships, 142, 153–64; with gay women, 164–65; not mixing business with, 144–48; with married men, 154–57; one-night stands, 165–67; swinging, 129
Shoes, 25, 34, 38–39, 80
Sickness, 140–42
Singles bars, 124, 125
Sleep, 132–33; jet lag and, 183–85
Small towns, 115–16
Snow, driving in the, 49–50
Speeds limits, 56–57

Stand-by procedure, 68–70
Stress, 137, 193
Suitcases, *see* Luggage
Swimming, 134–35
Swinging, 129

Tailgating, 50
Telephone calls home, 137–38
Television, 128
Theater, 123
Time zones, jet lag and, 183–85
Tips, 121–22
Tires, 44–45
Toilet items, 32
Travel agents, 66
Traveler's checks, 180
Truckers' motels, 87
Trucks, 58–59
Tune-ups, automobile, 54, 55

Vegetables, 98–100, 105, 106, 108; *See also* Salads
Vic Tanney clubs, 135

Wait-list, airline, 68–69
Windshield wipers, 50–51
Winter, driving in, 49–50

X-ray machines at airports, 34–35